Praise for the book

Selecting and Describing Your Research Instruments provides nice prototypes of letters, forms, worksheets, and content that can be easily used to augment course-specific content. This book helps the student and their research advisors by providing a thoughtful, step-by-step guide for moving through this vital yet underarticulated research component.

—**Elise Murowchick, PhD,** Lecturer, Psychology, Seattle University, Seattle, WA

Selecting and Describing Your Research Instruments

Concise Guides to Conducting Behavioral, Health, and Social Science Research Series

Conducting Your Literature Review
Susanne Hempel

Designing and Proposing Your Research Project
Jennifer Brown Urban and Bradley Matheus van Eeden-Moorefield

Managing Your Research Data and Documentation
Kathy R. Berenson

Selecting and Describing Your Research Instruments
Kelly S. McClure

Writing Your Psychology Research Paper
Scott A. Baldwin

Selecting and Describing Your Research Instruments

KELLY S. McCLURE

CONCISE GUIDES TO CONDUCTING BEHAVIORAL,
HEALTH, AND SOCIAL SCIENCE RESEARCH

 AMERICAN PSYCHOLOGICAL ASSOCIATION
PUBLISHING

Published by
American Psychological Association
750 First Street, NE
Washington, DC 20002
https://www.apa.org

Order Department
https://www.apa.org/pubs/books
order@apa.org

In the U.K., Europe, Africa, and the Middle East, copies may be ordered from Eurospan
https://www.eurospanbookstore.com/apa
info@eurospangroup.com

Typeset in Minion by Circle Graphics, Inc., Reisterstown, MD

Printer: Sheridan Books, Chelsea, MI
Cover Designer: Naylor Design, Washington, DC

Library of Congress Cataloging-in-Publication Data

Names: McClure, Kelly S., author.
Title: Selecting and describing your research instruments / Kelly S. McClure.
Description: Washington : American Psychological Association, 2020. |
   Series: Concise guides to conducting behavioral, health, and social
   science research | Includes bibliographical references and index.
Identifiers: LCCN 2020000547 (print) | LCCN 2020000548 (ebook) |
   ISBN 9781433832222 (paperback) | ISBN 9781433832239 (ebook)
Subjects: LCSH: Psychology—Research—Methodology. | Social sciences—
   Research—Methodology.
Classification: LCC BF76.5 .M3763 2020 (print) | LCC BF76.5 (ebook) |
   DDC 150.72—dc23
LC record available at https://lccn.loc.gov/2020000547
LC ebook record available at https://lccn.loc.gov/2020000548

http://dx.doi.org/10.1037/0000192-000

Printed in the United States of America

10 9 8 7 6 5 4 3 2 1

I dedicate this book to my grandmother, Lemoyne Paugh Sprague, who taught me a great deal about planning and organization. What she shared as life skills eventually developed into research skills as well.

Contents

CONTENTS

Series Foreword

Why are you reading this book? Perhaps you have been assigned to write a research paper in an undergraduate course. Maybe you are considering graduate school in one of the behavioral, health, or social science disciplines, such as psychology, public health, nursing, or medicine, and know that having a strong research background gives you a major advantage in getting accepted. Maybe you simply want to know how to conduct research in these areas. Or perhaps you are interested in actually conducting your own study. Regardless of the reason, you are probably wondering, "How do I start?"

Conducting research can be analogous to cooking a meal for several people. Doing so involves planning (e.g., developing a menu), having adequate resources (e.g., having the correct pots, pans, carving knives, plates), knowing what the correct ingredients are (e.g., what spices are needed), properly cooking the meal (e.g., grilling vs. baking, knowing how long it takes to cook), adequately presenting the food (e.g., making the meal look appetizing), and so forth. Conducting research also involves planning, proper execution, having adequate resources, and presenting one's project in a meaningful manner. Both activities also involve creativity, persistence, caring, and ethical behavior. But just like cooking a meal for several people, conducting research should follow one of my favorite pieces of advice, "Remember that the devil is in the details." If you want your dinner guests to find your meal tasty, you need to follow a recipe properly and measure the ingredients accurately (e.g., too much or little of various ingredients can make the entrée taste awful). Similarly, conducting research without properly paying attention to details can lead to erroneous results.

Okay, but what about your question, "How do I start?" This American Psychological Association book series provides detailed but user-friendly guides for conducting research in the behavioral, health, and social sciences from start to finish. I cannot help but think of another food analogy here—that is, the series will focus on everything from "soup to nuts." These short, practical books will guide you, the student/researcher, through each stage of the process of developing, conducting, writing, and presenting a research project. Each book focuses on a single aspect of research, such as choosing a research topic, following ethical guidelines when conducting research with humans, using appropriate statistical tools to analyze data, and deciding which measures to use in your project. Each volume in this series will help you attend to the details of a specific activity. All volumes will help you complete important tasks and include illustrative examples. Although the theory and conceptualization behind each activity are important to know, these books focus especially on the "how to" of conducting research, so that you, the research student, can successfully carry out a meaningful research project.

This volume, by Kelly McClure, focuses on identifying, choosing, and describing the most valid and appropriate research instruments and measures for your study. Continuing with the analogy of preparing a meal, you know that the quality of the needed ingredients can differ tremendously. For example, filet mignon far surpasses ground chuck. You are likely to suggest that there are vast differences across ice creams, coffee, donuts, and so forth (note that Prof. McClure uses a similar analogy, that of choosing the best musical instruments to use when playing a song). Choosing the correct instrument to measure a particular psychological construct is a critical factor when instructors and editors evaluate the validity of your study. McClure does a superb job in helping the reader to identify and define both the constructs and the means to measure such constructs. Moreover, she includes useful aids to enhance your ability to make this task stress-free, such as a checklist of steps to follow (Figure 1) and a compendium of key terms and definitions.

So, the answer to the question "How do I start?" is simple: Just turn the page and begin reading!

Best of luck!

—Arthur M. Nezu, PhD, DHL, ABPP
Series Editor

Acknowledgments

I thank Art Nezu for inviting me to participate in this series of Concise Guides. Art piqued my interested in the topic of instrument selection 20 years ago when we cowrote the *Practitioner's Guide to Empirically Based Measures of Depression* with George Ronan and Elizabeth Meadows (2010). Art was my main research mentor in graduate school and has continued to be a professional mentor for many years. I also want to thank Chris Nezu, another graduate research mentor who kindly stayed on as a professional mentor well beyond my time as a graduate student. I am especially grateful to Chris for being a valued female role model for me.

I also thank my students. Students are the heartbeat of my work. They inspire me every day to be the best that I can be. Their many curiosities and research inquiries are the foundation on which this book was developed. Special thanks to Amanda Chapin and Elle Markman for allowing me to use their studies as examples in this book.

There are several people to thank for helping me revise this book to produce the finished product you see today. Kristen Knight, American Psychological Association senior reference editor, was immensely helpful with editing. The anonymous reviewers provided invaluable feedback, and the production team made it a beautiful finished product.

Last, but certainly not least, I thank my home team: my husband Matt and my two sons Tim and Liam. They are simply the best. It means so much to have a family who believes in your work and supports what you do every day.

Selecting and Describing Your Research Instruments

Introduction

If you are reading this book, you may have an idea for a research study. You may have a research question in mind or even an idea of the method you would like to use. A *research question* is a broad question about the topic a researcher is studying. A *research method* is the methodical and scientific process a researcher uses to answer a research question. At whatever stage you find yourself in designing a study, the time has come to think more carefully about how you will measure the psychological or social science concepts you wish to study. This concise guide will provide all the information you need to choose the right instrument for your specific study. In psychology, *research instruments* are tools used to observe and describe psychological phenomena in a way that provides data that can be analyzed.

Have you ever watched a concert and seen the guitarist pick up a different guitar between songs or maybe even within the same song? This is

http://dx.doi.org/10.1037/0000192-001
Selecting and Describing Your Research Instruments, by K. S. McClure

because, in a concert, each instrument (in this example, a specific type of guitar) may produce a unique sound that best fits the song, the acoustics of the venue, the musicians in the band, or some combination of factors that impact how the audience experiences the music. Both guitars do the same basic job of making sounds by plucking and strumming strings. However, the fit of each guitar with a particular song is related to the goals of the musicians making the music. The same is true of research instruments in psychology and the social sciences. Instead of making music, in research you are asking questions about psychology or other social science concepts. It is critical that you select the best instrument to measure each concept you study.

You will have many choices to make about the research instruments you use for your study. For example, did you know that there are over 100 instruments available just to measure depression? Just like all guitars make music with strings, all these instruments measure depression. However, each instrument is designed for a specific type of goal, setting, format, or research participant. How does a researcher choose which instrument to use? New researchers are often surprised to learn that instrument selection is a complex and important step in the process of research design. This concise guide will show you how to identify the instruments that are available for your study, select the best instruments for the job, and describe the instruments so that others will know how and why you made your decisions. You may also find that the skills you develop and practice (e.g., goal setting, creating a detailed plan, creating and sticking to a timeline, digging deeper to find information, organizing large quantities of information, and collaborating) will transfer effectively to most jobs in a wide range of settings.

WHY AN ENTIRE GUIDE ON INSTRUMENT SELECTION?

If you were going to buy a guitar, you would probably gather some information about the different models and pricing before making your decision. The same is true for research instruments. All research instruments have limitations, and selecting the best instrument for a specific study requires weighing the instrument's strengths against its weaknesses for the specific task at hand. There is a lot to consider, including whether the instrument accurately measures the experiences and problems of the population with individual differences and diverse identities, languages, abilities, and other characteristics. Instrument selection is where researchers get to make some important choices that will impact the entire study, so it requires a careful and informed decision-making process. Unfortunately, if you do not give instrument selection some time and care, it may be difficult to interpret the results of your study later. I hope this guide will help you select the right instruments for the job before you collect and analyze your data so that you will be confident in your conclusions.

HOW TO USE THIS GUIDE

This guide is intentionally brief so that you can read it quickly and easily. Each chapter focuses on a specific aspect of instrument selection. It is designed to be read from beginning to end. There are a lot of examples to show you the concepts. There are also worksheets for you to fill out along the way. The worksheets are in the text, and I will explain when to use them. I recommend copying the worksheets so that you can use them again for your next study. (This may be the first study that you design, and hopefully, it is not your last!) You will get the most out of this guide if you complete the worksheets along the way. They will help you understand the concepts, keep track of your work, and document the steps you have taken while selecting your instruments. The worksheets are also designed to be communication tools, so take the completed worksheets to your advising meetings to help you explain the work you have done.

Research is best when it is conducted in a team. Building a team and consulting with an advisor is often a new skill for new researchers. As a research advisor, I have seen students get to the end of their projects before I realized that they did not fully consult with me. This step can slip through the cracks when students do not know what questions to ask, when to ask them, or when it is appropriate to reach out for consultation.

This brings us to your first exercise. Figure 1 provides a list of issues you should discuss with your advisor as you go through the process of selecting and describing your research instruments. It is meant to be filled out over time. Take a minute to read it now so that you are familiar with the issues you will discuss with your advisor. Then place a check next to Item 1 on the checklist to indicate that you reviewed the worksheet.

Advisor Consultation Checklist

Use the checklist below to ensure that you consulted with your advisor during the key steps in the process of selecting and describing your research instruments.

1. _____ Read this checklist
2. _____ Made an appointment for our first meeting to discuss the instrument selection
3. _____ Showed my advisor this checklist
4. _____ Reviewed Figure 1.2, The Present Study Research Question, Aim, and Hypotheses Worksheet
5. _____ Reviewed Figure 1.1, Examples of Study Constructs
6. _____ Reviewed Figure 3.1, Search Term Note-Taking Worksheet
7. _____ Discussed what languages the population of interest may speak
8. _____ Discussed accessibility considerations for the population of interest
9. _____ Reviewed Figure 4.2, Possible Instruments Note-Taking Worksheet
10. _____ Discussed permissions that will be required
11. _____ Reviewed Figure 6.1, Decision-Making Worksheet
12. _____ Discussed which demographic variables and whether confounding variables will be measured
13. _____ Discussed whether institutional review board (IRB) approval is required and, if applicable, how to apply
14. _____ Discussed potential grants to cover the cost of the study
15. _____ Discussed whether to develop an instrument if one does not exist
16. _____ Reviewed efforts to obtain permission when permissions could not be secured
17. _____ Reviewed the descriptions of the instruments for my study proposal
18. _____ Reviewed the descriptions of the instruments for my IRB application
19. _____ Reviewed the descriptions of the instruments for my final manuscript

---

Figure 1

Advisor consultation checklist.

As you work your way through this guide, check off each item that you complete in your Advisor Consultation Checklist.

This is also a good time to begin Item 2 on the Advisor Consultation Checklist. Contact your advisor to request a 15- to 30-minute appointment for a date 1 to 2 weeks from now. By then, you will have a few items to go over. I did not include reminders in the checklist to set every appointment with your advisor. Instead, I suggest setting up a regular meeting time to go over your instrument selection. Fifteen to 30 minutes every 2 weeks should be sufficient, and this can be done one-on-one or as part of a research group discussion.

The first two chapters in this guide discuss how to identify the constructs and variables and the types of instruments available for you to consider using in your studies. Some information in Chapters 1 and 2 will be familiar to you. I find it helpful to review these concepts frequently. Also, students usually find the information more meaningful when they are applying it to their own studies.

In Chapters 3 and 4, I show you how to identify what instruments are available, collect the specific information you need to select your instruments, how to organize the information and keep helpful notes that you can use later, and how to engage in a decision-making process to make your selection.

Then, in Chapters 5, 6, and 7, we walk through how to obtain permission to use the instruments, how to pilot them to test their feasibility, and ethical considerations. In Chapter 8, I show you how to write descriptions of these instruments for various audiences. Then, in Chapter 9, we go over troubleshooting many common challenges that arise during instrument selection. Finally, the book ends with a conclusion followed by definitions of important vocabulary terms found in the book with cross-references to the chapters where the terms are first used and defined in the text.

1

Identifying and Defining the Constructs and Variables to Measure

So you want to design a research study. There are so many interesting things to study in psychology and the social sciences. This book is about finding instruments to measure the topics you wish to study. Before we begin discussing instruments, though, let us make sure your research topic is clear and specific. It is important that you have a good idea of what you aim to study before you begin planning how you will measure those topics. If you are finding it difficult to choose your study topic, you are not alone. Beginning researchers often find it challenging to narrow down their study topics because there are so many good choices. If you have not narrowed down your topic yet, I recommend reading *Writing Your Psychology Research Paper* (Baldwin, 2018). Chapter 1 will guide you through the process of developing an idea, and the rest of the book is full of strategies for organizing your ideas until you arrive at a thesis.

It is important to remember that your study will take place within the larger context of social science research. Sticking with the music analogy

http://dx.doi.org/10.1037/0000192-002
Selecting and Describing Your Research Instruments, by K. S. McClure

from the Introduction, you can think of the body of social science research as a concert where each study is like one piece in the performance. One song on its own has meaning, but it has even more meaning when it is part of a set or a concert. Similarly, the findings from one study have meaning, but the meaning is even greater when the findings are part of a series of related or complementary studies. You can begin to understand how your study is part of a series of studies by conducting a thorough and critical review of the literature. Chapter 2 of *Writing Your Psychology Research Paper* (Baldwin, 2018) can help you with this process. Also, see *Conducting Your Literature Review* (Hempel, 2020), another guide in this series and one that focuses exclusively on the literature review. You should conduct the literature review before you select the research instruments for your study.

I also recommend that you develop one or two specific aims and one or two specific hypotheses and that you have these aims and hypotheses approved by your research advisor before you select your instruments. A *research aim* is the purpose or objective of a study. It sits within a trajectory of studies that collectively explain a psychological phenomenon or experience and is supported by a review of previous literature on the topic. A *hypothesis* is a proposition based on a theory or some limited evidence about the frequency of a phenomenon or how two or more variables are related. Table 1.1, Sample Research Questions, Aims, and Hypotheses, provides such examples for two hypothetical studies on posttraumatic growth in people with cancer. *Posttraumatic growth* is the personal growth that people sometimes experience after having gone through a trauma.

CONSTRUCTS

Constructs are so difficult to describe and define that philosophers and social scientists have been discussing what constructs are for decades (Lovasz & Slaney, 2013). Some of the early pioneers of psychological assessment defined *constructs* as theoretical concepts that "refer to the processes or entities that are not directly observed" (MacCorquodale & Meehl, 1948, p. 104) and attributes of people, "assumed to be reflected

	Table 1.1		
	Sample Research Question, Aim, and Hypothesis		
	Question	Aim	Hypothesis
Example 1	How often do adults with cancer experience personal growth after the diagnosis?	To understand the frequency with which adults with cancer experience posttraumatic growth.	More than 75% of adults with cancer will experience posttraumatic growth within the first year after diagnosis.
Example 2	Is posttraumatic growth related to lower stress in adults with cancer?	To understand the strength and direction of the relationship between posttraumatic growth and stress in adults with cancer.	There will be a statistically significant negative relationship between posttraumatic growth and stress in adults with cancer. Patients who experience more posttraumatic growth will report lower stress.

Note. It can be difficult to distinguish between a research question, an aim, and a hypothesis. This table provides two examples of possible questions, aims, and hypotheses for two different studies.

in test performance" (Cronbach & Meehl, 1955, p. 283). The American Psychological Association's *APA Dictionary of Psychology* (https://dictionary.apa.org/construct) defines a *construct* as "a complex idea or concept formed from a synthesis of simpler ideas."

Most research in psychology and social science studies constructs. Psychology researchers hold the idea or belief that attributes of people—attributes such as intelligence, happiness, and hope—exist even though we cannot feel, see, hear, touch, or smell them. However, researchers can measure these constructs so that their observations and descriptions of the constructs have meaning that can be understood by and communicated to others.

One helpful approach to identifying the constructs you aim to study is to find a published article that reports a study that is almost like the study you would like to conduct. You can find this in your literature review. There are empirical articles, which describe the purpose, method, results, and conclusions of one or a few studies. You can create a list of the constructs studied in all the empirical articles in your literature review. There is also a category of articles called systematic reviews and meta-analyses that review and synthesize all the articles on a specified topic. If a systematic review or meta-analysis has been conducted on the topic you wish to study, you are in luck because that article will list specific terms and constructs that the authors used to conduct their research on the topic. A *systematic review* is a type of literature review that includes a synthesis and summary of research on a particular topic to draw a new conclusion. A *meta-analysis* is a quantitative technique used to synthesize the results of studies that have already been conducted by conducting a mathematical analysis of the effect sizes of the studies.

Let us work through an example of how to identify constructs. I start by describing constructs that one of my students examined in her doctoral dissertation. I describe part of this study example here and then refer back to this study in Chapter 8 when discussing how to describe instruments for different audiences. This study was on the relationship between posttraumatic growth and social problem solving in adults with cancer and was eventually published in the *Journal of Clinical Psychology in Medical Settings* (Markman et al., 2019). The study examined two constructs: posttraumatic growth and social problem solving. As I mentioned earlier, posttraumatic growth is the personal growth that people sometimes experience after having gone through a trauma. *Social problem solving* is the methodical way people go about solving problems in their everyday lives. Although this study was conducted with adults with cancer, adults and cancer were not constructs examined. Adults with cancer is a description of the population of interest.

Let us work through another example together. This time, I describe the study, and you identify the constructs. The answers are in Figure 1.1, Examples of Study Constructs. This study was about student athletes. The issue or problem the student researcher identified was that student athletes experience about the same amount of mental health issues as students who are not on sports teams. However, student athletes seek help for their mental health issues less often than do other students who are not on athletic teams. This student decided to focus on whether

Examples of Study Constructs

Issue or problem	Construct
Study 1. Some adults with cancer experience personal growth after the experience of cancer and its treatment.	Posttraumatic growth
Individuals solve problems in a methodical way.	Social problem solving
Study 2. Student athletes have an identity as an athlete.	Athletic identity
This athletic identity may be related to student athlete attitudes about seeking help from the student counseling center or other mental health services when needed.	Mental health help-seeking attitudes

Figure 1.1

Examples of study constructs.

student athlete identities as athletes were related to their attitudes about seeking professional psychological help from the student counseling center or other mental health services when needed. The aim of the study was to understand whether athletic identity was related to student athletes' attitudes about seeking mental health treatment. The hypothesis was that student athletes who had strong identities as athletes would have more negative attitudes about seeking mental health treatment. What do you think are the two main constructs in this study?[1]

VARIABLE

Now that you understand what a construct is, let us also define what a variable is and then discuss how constructs and variables are similar and different. The *APA Dictionary of Psychology* (https://dictionary.apa.org/variable) defines a *variable* as "a condition in an experiment or a characteristic of an entity, person, or object that can take on different categories, levels, or values and that can be quantified (measured)." In research, variables are measured to describe the constructs under investigation.

---

[1] I acknowledge Elisabeth Markman and Amanda Chapin, who came up with these study ideas.

The construct is still abstract, whereas the variable is a measurable representation of that construct. Constructs and variables are similar in that they are both terms for ideas that are being studied. However, they are different in that the variable is a measurable representation of the construct. For example, social problem solving is a construct. When a person indicates how well they solve problems by stating, "I solve problems very well" or "I do not solve problems well at all," this is a variable. More specifically, this is a variable with two levels. Level 1 is "I solve problems very well," and Level 2 is "I do not solve problems very well at all." If we were to describe social problem solving as someone's score on a five-item questionnaire in which they rate each item on a scale of 1 to 5, social problem solving would be a variable with 25 levels (five items times five possible responses to each item).

There are two general types of variables: categorical and continuous. *Categorical variables* are variables that are described or measured in discrete or distinct categories. These may be nominal variables made up of two or more categories that do not have a distinct order, or ordinal variables that have two or more categories corresponding to the levels to indicate more or less of the variable but without a specific value to the level. *Continuous variables* are quantitative variables that, in theory, have an infinite number of values indicating the quantity or how much of the construct is present or reported by the participants.

In addition to understanding whether the variables are categorical or continuous, it will also help you understand whether you are measuring independent and dependent variables. These terms refer to the theories and hypotheses about how the variables are related when conducting an experiment. The *independent variables* are the variables that are manipulated or measured first to test how they influence the dependent variables. The *dependent variables* are the variables that you believe are being affected by the independent variables. Whether the variables are independent or dependent will not have much influence on which instruments you select. However, if you are conducting an experiment, knowing what the independent and dependent variables are in your study will help ensure that you select an instrument for every variable that has to be measured.

OPERATIONAL DEFINITIONS

Each variable in your study will need an operational definition. *Operational definitions* are the specific methods by which the variables are observed and measured in a particular study. The rest of this book will guide you through the process of deciding on an operational definition for each variable in your study. In our example of the posttraumatic growth and social problem-solving study, there are many ways the researcher could measure posttraumatic growth and social problem solving. For example, each variable could be measured by asking participants to answer a series of questions related to their growth after cancer and how they solve problems. The questions could be about posttraumatic growth and social problem solving in general, or they could be about growth specifically after cancer and approaches to solving problems about cancer and treatment. These variables and operational definitions, as well as issues to consider, are demonstrated in Table 1.2.

There is one more thing to consider: You may also have to measure confounding variables. These are not the main variables in your hypotheses. The *main variables* are the variables related to the study's aims and hypotheses. The main variables are often the variables you are most interested in for a specific study. *Confounding variables* are variables that may make it difficult to understand the results of a study because they also help to explain the relationship between the two variables of interest by offering an alternative explanation as to why the variables are related. A *demographic variable* is a variable that describes the personal characteristics of an individual (e.g., age, race, religion). Sometimes a demographic variable is also a confounding variable. Sometimes, a demographic variable is used simply to describe the participants in a study. This guide focuses on the main variables in your study. If you are measuring confounding or demographic variables, you will need good instruments for these variables too. You may have to consult with your advisor about which confounding or demographic variables to measure. You will use the same process that is described in this guide to select instruments to measure these variables. I recommend focusing on selecting the instruments to measure the main variables for your current study

Table 1.2
Variables and Operational Definitions Example

Variable	Possible operational definitions	Issues to consider
Posttraumatic growth	1. An individual's score on the Posttraumatic Growth Inventory (Tedeschi & Calhoun, 1996), with higher scores indicating more posttraumatic growth and lower scores indicating less posttraumatic growth. 2. Responses to an interview asking participants to describe their growth over the past year when they have been undergoing cancer treatment.	Each of the possible operational definitions is an example of an acceptable operational definition of posttraumatic growth. The researcher has to decide whether it is most important to measure general posttraumatic growth with a measure that is already developed and offers the ability to compare scores with those from other studies (in which Operational Definition 1 would be a better choice) or to specifically measure posttraumatic growth after cancer (in which Operational Definition 2 would be better).
Social problem solving	1. An individual's score on the self-report questionnaire, the Social Problem-Solving Inventory–Revised (D'Zurilla, Nezu, & Maydeu-Olivares, 2002), with higher scores indicating more effective social problem-solving skills. 2. Score on a performance test that requires participants to solve a problem while being observed.	Operational Definition 1 offers a quicker measure of social problem solving, however it relies on the person's assessment of how well they solve problems. Operational Definition 2 does not rely on the person's self-assessment but requires more human resources (time from the participants and the observer, plus observer training) and may be less applicable to social problems if the performance task is more general.

first and then moving on to selecting the instruments for the confounding or demographic variables. Figure 1 includes an item for consulting with your advisor about measuring confounding or demographic variables.

Now, try to think of the research question, aim, and hypotheses for your study. In a published paper about a study, the authors refer to that study as the *present study*. Therefore, in Table 1.2, I refer to the study that you are currently designing as the *present study*. Figure 1.2, the present study research question, aim, and hypotheses worksheet, provides a

The Present Study Research Question, Aim, and Hypotheses Worksheet

Research question	Aim	Hypotheses (limit the study to 1–3 hypotheses)
		Hypothesis 1:
		Hypothesis 2 (if applicable):
		Hypothesis 3 (if applicable):

Figure 1.2

The present study research question, aim, and hypotheses worksheet.

worksheet for you to write down the question, aims, and hypotheses of the study you are currently designing. Fill this out now as best you can. In your next appointment, go over this completed worksheet to make sure that your question, aim, and hypotheses are clear, so you and your advisor agree about what they should be. After the meeting, make any needed revisions to Figure 1.2. Then check off Item 4 on your Advisor Consultation Checklist. Now that your research question, aim, and hypothesis or hypotheses are clear, let us move on to constructs and variables, which is the topic you will discuss with your advisor in the meeting after you discuss the question, aims, and hypotheses.

SUMMARY

This chapter focused on identifying and defining the constructs and variables to measure. Before selecting the instruments you will use for your study, it is important that you know the aims and hypotheses of your study, paying particular attention to the type of claim you intend to examine. Figure out how many constructs you wish to measure for your study and identify which are the independent and dependent variables in the study. You will need an instrument to measure each measured variable in your study.

2

Types of Instruments and Their Properties: Methods to Measure Variables and Constructs

Now that you know which constructs and variables you are studying, let us spend some time discussing what options may be available to you with regard to instruments. In this chapter, I begin by describing the types of instruments available to you. I then discuss the psychometric properties of an instrument, which I define later in this chapter.

TYPES OF INSTRUMENTS

Types of instruments fall into four general categories: self-report, interview, observational, and physiological. In this chapter, I describe each category and the benefits and drawbacks of each type of instrument. I also describe activity trackers, which are newer technologies that do not fall neatly into the four traditional instrument categories but are worth mentioning because of their growing popularity. I then conclude with a discussion about the benefits and drawbacks of using multiple types of

http://dx.doi.org/10.1037/0000192-003
Selecting and Describing Your Research Instruments, by K. S. McClure

instruments to measure the same construct in the same study. In this chapter, I use the examples of how to measure sleep or aspects of sleep using the different instrument categories. It is important to note that these are all examples of individual data. You may also find that you use other types of data such as grades in a school setting or cancer stages in a health psychology setting that do not fall into these four categories of instruments.

Self-Report Instruments

A *self-report instrument* is an instrument that an individual completes by answering questions about him- or herself. The questions may be provided in a variety of formats. An open-ended format poses a question and allows individuals to respond any way they wish. For example, an open-ended self-report question may be "Describe how well you slept last night." A forced-response format, however, provides specific options for responding, and individuals choose the response that best describes their experience. A forced response question may ask individuals to indicate on a five-point scale the extent to which they agree with a particular statement. For example, instructions may say, "Indicate how much you agree with the following statement: I slept very well last night." The individual must choose one of five answers that range from *disagree strongly* to *agree strongly*. This is a specific type of forced-choice format called a *Likert scale*. Forced choice formats may also offer true/false or yes/no options for responding.

Regardless of the format, self-report instruments collect information about individuals' perceptions of their experiences. This type of instrument is particularly useful when conducting research on emotions or thoughts that only an individual can describe about him- or herself. The drawback of this type of instrument, though, is that the level, intensity, or frequency of one's experience is subjective. What I describe as sleeping well, and what you describe as sleeping well may not be the same. When using self-report instruments, it is essential that the researcher keeps in mind that the information collected describes individuals' perceptions of their experiences. Open-ended formats also require the researcher to develop a scoring rubric to compare and categorize responses from different participants. This can be time consuming, both in developing the rubric and scoring the responses by interpreting how each response fits in the rubric.

Interviews

Interview instruments are exactly what the name implies: The researcher interviews participants and records their responses. There are three general interview formats: unstructured, semi-structured, and structured. *Unstructured* interviews pose questions and allow the participants to respond however they choose. For example, the interviewer may say, "Describe how you slept last night." *Semi-structured* interviews provide a little more guidance to the interviewer by offering narrower questions, as well as specific information to follow up on once the participants provide their initial responses. If a participant responds with, "I slept terribly," a semi-structured interview may prompt the interviewers to ask the participant to define *terribly* and prompt them for details such as the length of time slept, how restless the sleep was, or how many times they woke up throughout the night. The third type of interview is a *structured* interview. In this type of interview, the researcher asks specific questions and does not go off script to ask follow-up questions.

The benefit of an interview is that the researcher can dig a little deeper for specific details about a person's experience. The interview also allows the researcher to clarify any vague or confusing responses. The drawback is that the researcher's hypotheses about the study may inadvertently influence the way they ask questions or record responses. This bias can be countered a bit by keeping the interviewers unaware of the study hypotheses. However, this is not always possible. The researchers' biases about the individual participants also may implicitly bias how they ask questions or record responses. This can be countered by training interviewers to be aware of their implicit biases. This cannot counter all implicit biases, but it is one approach that should be used for multi-culturally competent research.

Interview methods of instrumentation require a lot of time for several reasons. First, the interviews themselves take time. Second, the interviewers must be trained to build rapport with the interviewees while remaining professional, and they must be trained to follow a protocol so that each interview is conducted in a similar manner. Unstructured interviews require a rubric for scoring, extensive training for those scoring the interviews, and a lot of time. Semi-structured interviews also require a rubric and time; however, they are less time consuming than unstructured interviews. Researchers also have to consider whether the interviews will be recorded and, if so, how and where the recordings are stored so that the identity and personal information of the participants are protected.

Observational Instruments

Observational measures are instruments that a researcher completes while observing participants engaging in a particular behavior or several behaviors. The researcher begins by defining the behavior to be measured. For example, the researcher studying sleep may decide to observe how many hours each participant slept. The definition could be made even more specific by defining hours slept as the number of minutes that pass between when participants close their eyes and when they open them. The researcher then sets the conditions for the observation. For example, the observation may take place in participants' homes through a video recording device. Alternatively, the observation may take place in a sleep laboratory where participants spend the night, making in-person observation easier and a little less intrusive to the participants.

Observational instruments require specific operational definitions. They also require the researcher to decide whether the observations will take place in a natural setting (e.g., observing sleep at home) or in a more controlled setting that will be similar for each participant (e.g., in a lab). The observers also have to be trained so that (a) they are recording what the research study intends to measure, and (b) if there are multiple observers, they measure and record the same observations in the same way. For example, if I am told to record the time that elapses between when someone closes his eyes and when he opens them, and the participant closes his eyes and then opens them 10 minutes later to adjust his position, I may record that as the time slept. However, another person may not count that as time slept and may simply count from the time the eyes close in the evening and when they open again in the morning. Multiple observers have to agree on how they are going to measure and record what they see. The drawback to observational measures is that training the recorders is time consuming, and there is the chance that internal validity will be compromised if observers interpret and record observations differently. The benefit of observational measures is that they are not influenced by the perceptions or biases of the participants.

Physiological Instruments

Physiological instruments observe and record physiological activity in the body. Physiological activities that are commonly measured in psychological research are heart rate, blood pressure, brain activity, and metabolic function. In a study on sleep, a researcher may use an electroencephalogram (EEG) to measure variations in brain waves that correspond to particular phases of sleep. The benefit of physiological measures is that they are not impacted by participant or observer bias. However, there are several drawbacks. Physiological instruments can be expensive, as can the training required for researchers to properly use the instruments. The instruments may require maintenance or upgrading as new technology is developed, creating additional and ongoing costs. Some participants may find physiological measures to be too invasive and may elect not to participate in the study. Moreover, although physiological measures may record the same physiological activity across participants, different participants may experience that physiological activity differently. For example, two individuals may have similar sleep patterns in their EEG output, but one person may report that she slept well, and the other may report that she slept poorly.

Activity Trackers and Wearable Technology

There is a growing interest in using *activity trackers and wearable technology* to collect social science data. These are technological devices typically bought through consumer markets (i.e., from a retailer and not from a physician). Activity trackers, such as those sold by Fitbit, are specifically for tracking activity. Wearable technology, such as the Apple Watch, is designed as an accessory and may include an activity tracking function along with other features such as texting, music, and so forth. Either way, when these devices include an activity-tracking function, they may record a variety of activities such as steps taken, hours slept, and other physical activity behaviors. Although they are marketed for consumers to monitor their activities, researchers can use activity trackers and wearable technology as research instruments as well. For example, a researcher studying a new public health information campaign that shows the benefits of walking more may use activity trackers to measure the average number of steps the participants take before and after being exposed to the information.

If you are considering using an activity tracker or wearable technology, I recommend being cautious for several reasons. First, these instruments were developed for the mass market and not specifically for psychological research. Second, it can be confusing to figure out what type of data are being collected. For example, the count of the number of steps people take is observational data, but because it is being collected in an electronic device that is worn on the body, it can seem like physiological data. If you are going to use data from an activity tracker, you have to be clear about what you are truly measuring. Third, the psychometric properties of these instruments are not well documented (Evenson, Goto, & Furberg, 2015). This is a good time to review psychometric properties. But first, let us consider an example illustrating some of the previous points.

In this example, let us say that I wanted to do a study on activity levels of children during school. Activity level during school is the variable. Table 2.1 lists a variety of ways in which the variable of activity level during school can be measured using the various types of instruments. You will see that each type of instrument offers a unique measure of the variable. The table lists some pros and cons for each type of instrument to measure this variable. You might think of other pros and cons that are not in the table. The pros and cons of instruments are unique for each variable.

Table 2.1

Types of Instruments to Measure Activity Levels of Children in Schools

Instrument type	Example	Pros and cons
Self-report	The children can complete a questionnaire about how often they move around during their classes. Alternatively, the teachers could complete a questionnaire about how often the children move around during their lessons.	Pros: standard questions and responses for each person; children and teachers can report Cons: they may over- or underreport how often the children move
Interview	The researchers can interview the children, the teachers, or both to ask how often the children move around during their classes. The interviews can be done one-on-one or in small groups.	Pros: responses may provide more detail; children and teachers can report Cons: coding the responses will take time
Observational	The researchers can sit in the classrooms and observe segments of the class. They can use a checklist of potential behaviors (e.g., talking, getting out of seat, walking around) and check off which behaviors they observe.	Pros: specific behaviors can be counted Cons: only parts of the day will be observed; children may change their behavior if they know they are being observed
Physiological	The researchers can measure the heart rate of the children, with the assumption that higher heart rates are related to higher activity levels.	Pros: standard measurement Cons: heart rate may not be a valid measure of activity
Activity tracker	The children can wear Fitbits during school and track the number of steps that they take throughout the school day.	Pros: standard measure for each person Cons: cost; steps are only one component of activity; children may change their number of steps in response to wearing a new device (but they can wear it for a while and acclimate to it before the researchers begin recording the data)

Note. This table lists some possible types of instruments that could measure activity levels of children in school as well as some pros and cons of each type of instrument to measure this variable.

PSYCHOMETRIC PROPERTIES

As I mentioned at the beginning of this chapter, it is important to consider the psychometric properties of the instruments when you consider which instrument to use. The *psychometric properties* of an instrument are the data that have been collected about an instrument to help us understand how well the instrument measures the construct. The psychometric properties of instruments fall into two general categories: reliability and validity.

Reliability

Reliability refers to the consistency with which a construct is measured across various contexts and/or populations. Researchers can test the reliability of an instrument using a few different methods. There are three reliability scores you are likely to come across.

The first type of reliability is *internal reliability* (also sometimes called *internal consistency reliability*). This type of reliability is typically used for questionnaires to show how well each item is related to the total score of that questionnaire. Cronbach's alpha is the statistical test used to test internal reliability, and you will see it reported in papers with the symbol α. Cronbach's alpha scores range from 0 to 1. In general, you should try to use an instrument with a Cronbach's alpha score ranging from .7 to .9. For a longer discussion of how to interpret Cronbach's alpha, see Tavakol and Dennick (2011).

The second type of reliability is *test–retest reliability*. This is a type of reliability that shows that an instrument administered multiple times to the same group of people will consistently measure results every time. This type of reliability helps a researcher understand the stability of the construct over time. It is particularly important for study designs, such as longitudinal research, that require researchers to measure a construct repeatedly over time. The statistical test typically used to examine test–retest reliability is a correlation, with scores ranging from 0 to 1, where higher scores indicate better reliability.

The third type of reliability is *alternate-forms reliability*. This is when two equivalent forms are developed to test the same construct, and the forms are correlated. The statistical test typically used to examine alternate-forms reliability is also a correlation, with scores ranging from 0 to 1, where higher scores indicate better reliability. Alternate forms are sometimes used in repeated measures designs to prevent *testing effects* (when taking the test a second time affects the score not because the variable has changed but because the participants have gotten used to the test or have become tired from the test). Administering an equivalent but a slightly different form of the test in follow-up administrations will counter testing effects.

Validity

Validity describes how well an instrument measures the construct the researcher intends to measure. There are four main types of validity. Interpreting the statistical tests for validity is more complicated than interpreting reliability results. Consult with your advisor to make sure you have an accurate understanding of the information about the validity of the measures you are selecting. However, let us review the main types of validity that are measured in research instruments.

Predictive validity describes how strongly an instrument is related to or correlates with something that it is supposed to be measuring. Predictive validity is specific, though, in that it describes the correlation between the instrument and some other method of measuring the same construct at a later point.

Concurrent validity, however, describes how strongly an instrument correlates with some other method of measuring the same construct at the same time. Predictive and concurrent validity are both *criterion-related validity* because they examine the correlation between the instrument and a specified criterion. The only difference is that predictive validity measures the criterion at a later point, and concurrent validity measures the criterion at the same time the instrument is administered.

Content validity is the degree to which the instrument measures the entire construct being studied. Let us return to the example of the study on mental health issues in student athletes from Figure 1.1 in Chapter 1 to further explain content validity. If the instrument measuring mental health issues measures anxiety but no other types of mental health issues, there may be some limits to the content validity of that instrument for that study. This is because mental health issues include many other things in addition to anxiety.

Finally, *construct validity* is the degree to which the instrument measures the construct the researcher thinks it is measuring. I recall a poorly designed study that determined that my city was the most overweight city in the United States. One of the ways the study measured whether the people in the city were overweight was by counting the number of pizza shops there were per square mile. Our city happens to be densely populated and has a lot of people of Italian descent, making the number of pizza shops per square mile quite high. To me, this "instrument" seemed to measure the number of Italian Americans and population density more than the number of overweight people. I was not convinced that this instrument had good construct validity.

MULTITRAIT–MULTIMETHOD APPROACH, MULTIPLE INSTRUMENTS, AND PARTS OF INSTRUMENTS

The multitrait–multimethod approach (Eid et al., 2008) uses multiple methods to evaluate the psychometric properties of a construct. This is a complex approach that you should be aware exists. However, I would not expect that you would use this approach in your first research study. It involves a process of considering all the data available from the literature to determine the psychometric properties of an instrument. If you are considering the multitrait–multimethod approach, be sure to discuss it with your research advisor because you will likely need assistance with the data analysis.

No single instrument can measure a psychological construct perfectly or exactly. Ideally, a researcher should use multiple methods of measurement. For example, a study on sleep may use a participant self-report instrument, an observational measure, and an activity tracker. Then the similarities and differences between the results when using the different instrumentation methods can be compared and contrasted. However, using multiple methods requires more time and money. In Chapter 6, I go into more detail about how to weigh the benefits and drawbacks of using more than one instrument to measure a construct.

Sometimes new researchers want to use parts of instruments in their studies. Although this seems like an attractive idea because it offers shorter instruments, whenever researchers modify research instruments, they risk changing the reliability and validity of the instruments as well. The best way to ensure that the psychometric properties of the instruments are preserved is to administer the instruments in the form in which they were created.

SUMMARY

This chapter focused on the types of instruments psychology and social science researchers use to measure variables and constructs. The main types of instruments are self-report, interview, observational, and physiological. As you prepare to look for available instruments, it is important to know what psychometric properties are and how they inform the usefulness of each instrument. The psychometric property of reliability refers to whether the instrument produces similar data every time the construct is measured, and the psychometric property of validity refers to whether the data from an instrument accurately represent the construct being measured. Soon, when you choose the instruments for your study, the psychometric properties of the instruments will factor into your decisions.

3

Identifying Available Instruments

There are often several options available for measuring each construct. How does a researcher find out what the options are? Although your first thought may be to begin with a broad search tool such as Google, other approaches are more efficient and produce more accurate and detailed results. In this chapter, I describe three main approaches for identifying how the constructs to be studied have already been measured. The first approach is to use library databases and search engines. I describe some of those tools and how to use them. The chapter will also include a few detailed examples. The second approach is to use books and book chapters on instruments. The third approach is to search the methods sections of the empirical studies that have informed the study. I provide an example of how to look at the method section of journal articles to find instruments. The chapter concludes with some tips on consulting with librarians,

http://dx.doi.org/10.1037/0000192-004
Selecting and Describing Your Research Instruments, by K. S. McClure

experts, and your advisor when identifying available instruments. The next chapter addresses gathering and organizing your information.

LIBRARY DATABASES AND SEARCH ENGINES

A *library database* is an electronic catalog that contains published works in a particular field. A *search engine* is a tool that can be used to find materials in a database by searching for user-provided keywords. You likely can access many library databases and search engines through your university library website. If you have not done so already, visit your university library to set up an account and find out the best way to access the library databases remotely. That way, you can get the best results from your database searches. For example, our university library requires a password to access the databases from an off-campus computer. Furthermore, searching our library databases works more effectively on some Internet browsers than others. Our librarians recommend using Firefox to search our library from off campus, but every campus is different, so check with your librarian.

Once you know the best way to access the library resources and you have your account and password, you should choose a few of those tools to use. The following are a few databases and search engines that may be particularly useful for helping you select your instruments. The list is organized from the broadest to the narrowest database. Once you select a database to search, you will also have to know how to search that database. The most common resources for searching for instruments are described in this section as well as in Table 3.1.

Comprehensive Search Tools

Some libraries offer comprehensive search tools such as an omnibox or a product called Summon. These comprehensive tools search multiple content databases at once. This type of tool will provide the broadest results. However, when looking for instruments, they will often provide such broad results that it will be time consuming to find what you are looking for.

Table 3.1

Resources Finding Instruments

Database or book	Benefits	Drawbacks
Summon	Searches from a broad range of databases	May provide more information than you need
APA PsycInfo	Searches psychology publications	May provide references to articles in which the instrument is used, making it difficult to isolate articles specifically about the instrument's reliability and validity
Google Scholar	Free to use and accessible to anyone with internet access	Difficult to identify articles most relevant to your study
Health and Psychosocial Instruments	Specifically searches for instruments; primary sources are easier to identify	Not available in all libraries; limited number of simultaneous users
APA PsycTests	In addition to the bibliographic information, provides the actual test or test items for about 50% of the instruments in the database. In addition, you can subscribe directly to this database through the American Psychological Association.	There is a subscription fee if your library does not subscribe.
Mental Measurements Yearbook	Includes reviews of the instruments by qualified professionals to help you evaluate the benefits and drawbacks of each instrument	Provides information about all known tests, so it will include tests of variables that you are not studying
ABCT Clinical Assessment Series	Thorough and detailed information	Only related to measures for specific constructs
Handbooks	May have a chapter on the measurement of a particular construct	Only available for specific constructs; may need to order through interlibrary loan if it is not in your library's collection

APA PsycInfo

APA PsycInfo is an abstracting and indexing database for literature in the behavioral sciences and mental health. There are millions of records in APA PsycInfo, most of which are peer-reviewed journal articles, book chapters, books, and technical reports. Searching APA PsycInfo for instruments provides more narrow or specific results than a search in Summon because it is limited to publications in behavioral science and mental health. However, the results still provide records for publications that may not specifically focus on an instrument. The results provide records that include the title, authors, source, language, key words, and abstract. Probably the most useful part of the records is "Tests and Measures," which lists all the instruments that were used in a particular study and the digital object identifier (DOI). The DOI is an alphanumeric string assigned to content, including electronic books and research articles. Publishers, in consultation with a registration agency called the International DOI Foundation, assign a unique DOI to an article when it is published. Each DOI begins with a 10 and contains a prefix and a suffix separated by a slash (American Psychological Association [APA], 2010). For example, http://dx.doi.org/10.1007/b108176 is the DOI for the *Practitioners' Guide to Empirically Based Measures of Anxiety* (Antony, Orsillo, & Roemer, 2001). You can enter a DOI into a search engine to search for a specific publication. Most modern articles have a DOI. However, some older articles might not have a DOI. If the library owns an electronic copy of the article, the DOI in the database usually provides a link to the full electronic article. APA PsycInfo is different than APA PsycArticles. APA PsycArticles is a database that is limited to full-text peer-reviewed articles published by the APA and affiliated journals. APA PsycInfo offers a broader search for measures than APA PsycArticles.

Google Scholar

Google Scholar is a tool developed by Google that can also be used to identify articles about psychology and social science instruments. The main benefits of using Google Scholar to search for instruments are that it is free to use, is accessible to anyone with Internet access, and searches a broad range of scholarly literature in one place. Google Scholar ranks the articles using criteria such as the reputation of the author and the number of times the article has been cited. Although this information is helpful in general, it will not help you identify whether there is a good fit between the variables and the possible instruments for your study. One drawback to using Google Scholar for instrument selection is that it will identify many different types of publications, which may make it difficult to identify the articles most relevant to your study.

Health and Psychosocial Instruments

Health and Psychosocial Instruments (HaPI) specifically contains records on behavioral measurement instruments. The collection in HaPI includes psychological instruments as well as other behavioral measurement instruments that may be used in health and allied health professions, such as nursing and physical therapy. You can search HaPI with a keyword or phrase, author, article title, or journal title. Search results provide records that include the title of the instrument, acronym, and authors. The record also has a section called "Source Code," which indicates whether the record is a primary source. A *primary source* for an instrument is a manuscript that reports the original study about an instrument, such as the development and properties of the instrument. In contrast, a *secondary source* about an instrument is an article or book that may include a description of the instrument, but that is not the main purpose of the publication. In addition, the record has a section called "References" that provides a reference to the primary source. I find the organization of the records in HaPI to be particularly helpful when I am trying to find the primary source that describes an instrument and when I am trying to obtain a copy of the instrument. The primary source often provides a copy of the instrument or instructs the reader about how to access the instrument.

For example, I opened HaPI and typed the word *depression* in the text box and clicked "Search." The search produced many records regarding instruments to measure depression. The seventh record on the list was entitled "Patient Health Questionnaire for Anxiety and Depression." When I clicked the link to that record, I could see that the acronym for this instrument is PHQ-4, and the source of this record was a secondary source about a study on managing depression among diverse older adults in primary care (Emery-Tiburcio et al., 2017). The record also provided a reference to Kroenke, Spitzer, Williams, and Löwe (2009), which probably provides a more detailed description of the PHQ-4. If I want to know more about the PHQ-4, I will go to my library catalog and obtain a copy of the Kroenke et al. (2009) article.

One thing to note about HaPI is that libraries may hold a limited subscription to this database, which means that only a limited number of users from the same university can access HaPI at the same time. If your university has a subscription to HaPI and you cannot open it, wait an hour and try again. If you still cannot open it, see your librarian.

APA PsycTests

APA PsycTests is a database produced by the APA and is available through most university libraries. It provides a collection of tens of thousands of records about psychological tests, measures, assessments, and surveys. You can find more information about this database at http://www.apa.org/pubs/databases/psyctests. If you do not have access to a library database, you can also purchase a subscription to APA PsycTests directly from the APA. In addition to providing descriptions about the measures, this database has copies of about 50% of the instruments in the collection.

Select a Search Term or Search Terms

In addition to selecting a database for your search, you also have to select a search term to enter into the database. For example, if I am doing a study on happiness, and I would like to measure the construct "happiness," I can type the word *happiness* into the search box in any selected database. When I type *happiness* into HaPI, a few instruments that are listed in the results are the Savoring Beliefs Inventory, Subjective Happiness

Scale, Quality of Life Profile, and Apparent Emotions Scale. This tells me that some other terms that may help me find an instrument to measure happiness are savoring beliefs, quality of life, and apparent emotions. Then, when I click on the link to the record for the Subjective Happiness Scale because that term seems to be closest to what I am looking for, there is a section called "Measures Descriptors," which lists other terms to help me search. In this example, the measures descriptors are "Emotional States," "Emotions," and "Happiness." To identify the broadest list of instruments that may be available to measure happiness, I may want to search the database with all three of these terms.

A second way to identify search terms is to look at a few articles. Research articles in psychology are structured consistently so that researchers can search and store the information effectively. Within this structure, a few key words are generally listed under the abstract in every article. If you already have an article that informed the aims or hypotheses of the study that you are designing, it is a good idea to look for the keywords listed under the abstract and use those when you search the library database for instruments. After you enter the search term that you selected, you may also find it useful to type the word *psychometric* as a second keyword in your search because this term may help the database or search engine narrow down the search to articles that are about instruments.

BOOKS AND BOOK CHAPTERS

In addition to library databases and search engines, there are also books that can assist you in your search for instruments. Some books about instruments cover a broad range of topics that researchers can measure. Other books go into depth on specific topics to measure. This section describes a few of each.

Mental Measurements Yearbook

The *Mental Measurements Yearbook* is published every 3 years by the Buros Center for Testing, an organization that publishes reference materials about testing and assessment and provides other services related to instrument use and development. The 20th yearbook was produced in 2017 (Carlson, Geisinger, & Jonson, 2017). The yearbook contains full-text information about all English-language standardized tests covering educational skills, personality, vocational aptitude, psychology, and related areas. The *Mental Measurements Yearbook* also contains reviews of the measures. You may be able to access an electronic version of the *Mental Measurements Yearbook* online through your university database catalog, and you can search the yearbook using search terms much like those you would search for in other databases. Print versions of the *Mental Measurements Yearbook* may also be available in the library.

The Association for Behavioral and Cognitive Therapies Clinical Assessment Series

Springer published the Association for Behavioral and Cognitive Therapies (ABCT) Clinical Assessment series in collaboration with the ABCT, a professional organization that promotes the scientific understanding of human problems through broad applications of behavioral, cognitive, and biological principles (abct.org). The series includes five books that are practitioner's guides to empirically based measures of anger, aggression, and violence (Ronan, Dreer, Maurelli, Ronan, & Gerhart, 2014); school behavior (Kelley, Reitman, & Noell, 2003); social skills (Nangle, Hansen, Erdley, & Norton, 2010); depression (Nezu, Ronan, Meadows, & McClure, 2000); and anxiety (Antony, Orsillo, & Roemer, 2001). These books are available in print or as e-books. Each book provides a thorough list of measures on the topic. Each description includes information about the purpose of the measures, validity and reliability, when or how it has been used either in practice or research, references to the original source of the measure, and copyright information. The books also contain copies of many of the instruments. If you are studying any of the topics covered by these books, you will find the books to be invaluable tools in selecting your instrument.

Handbooks

There are handbooks on some subject areas, especially in clinical psychology. For example, there is the *Handbook of Depression* (Gotlib & Hammen, 2015). These handbooks provide the most up-to-date information about the construct and often have a chapter on measurement. A chapter such as this will provide descriptions of many of the instruments available to measure those constructs. If you use a handbook to identify instruments, be sure to note the handbook publication date and look for any new instruments that were published after the handbook was published. Table 3.1 provides a summary of the benefits and drawbacks of the approaches described in this chapter so far.

ARTICLE SEARCHING

Another approach to identifying instruments is to look at articles that have already been published. Go back to your literature review and select one to three articles that describe a study examining a research question similar to the one you are asking. There are three approaches to examining these articles that may help you identify good instruments for your study: method section, backward reference, and backward author searching. Most people use a combination of these article searching approaches to identify instruments for their studies.

When using article searches, it is important to create an organized method for recording the results. I recommend taking notes on a worksheet, such as the one provided in Figure 3.1. When searching for instruments, this tool will be used mostly for article searches, but it can be used for other types of searches as well. You may have to search more later, and your notes will help you continue the search without repeating what you have already done.

Method Section Searching

The method section of the article(s) includes descriptions of all instruments used in the study. I often tell my students that this is the section of

---

Search Term Note-Taking Worksheet

Variable 1

1. What is the name of the variable you wish to measure?

_____

2. List the search terms you will enter into the databases to look for instruments that measure this variable.

_____

3. List the resources from Table 3.1 you will use to look for instruments that measure this variable.

_____

Variable 2

1. What is the name of the variable you wish to measure?

_____

2. List the search terms you will enter into the databases to look for instruments that measure this variable.

_____

3. List the resources from Table 3.1 you will use to look for instruments that measure this variable.

_____

Variable 3

1. What is the name of the variable you wish to measure?

_____

2. List the search terms you will enter into the databases to look for instruments that measure this variable.

_____

3. List the resources from Table 3.1 you will use to look for instruments that measure this variable.

_____

Figure 3.1

Search term note-taking worksheet.

a paper you are probably tempted to skip when you are reading to find out the conclusion. However, it is an important section to read if you want to understand and critique the validity of the study. It is also an important section to read if you are looking for instruments to measure the same or similar constructs. The paper will include a paragraph describing the format, validity, and reliability of the instrument as well as references to other papers that describe these instruments. These other papers are

IDENTIFYING AVAILABLE INSTRUMENTS

called primary sources because they are the original papers that describe the development of the instruments. It is important to read the primary source that describes each instrument you intend to use.

Backward Reference Searching

Another way you can identify possible instruments for your study is to go through the reference section of the one to three articles you selected from your literature review and identify any additional articles that may be particularly relevant to your study. Obtain a copy of these additional articles and then search the method section of those articles to see which instruments the authors used.

Backward Author Searching

In addition to searching the reference section of the one to three articles you identified from your literature review, you can search the authors of those studies to see whether they conducted any other studies on the topic and, if so, which instruments they used in the other studies. To conduct a backward author search, you can use a database or search engine such as APA PsycInfo or the others that were described earlier in this chapter. Type the author's name in the search box and then use the drop-down menu to indicate you are looking for an author. From the results of this search, look at the instruments lists of the articles that also study the same construct. You may find that some authors tend to use the same instruments in many of their studies.

CONSULT

It can be helpful to consult with several people while you are searching for available instruments. Getting as many experts to weigh in on whether you have considered every option helps ensure that you have conducted a complete and thorough search. Librarians and your advisor may be particularly helpful.

Librarian

In this chapter alone, I have already suggested that you visit your librarian at least twice. I cannot emphasize enough how helpful university librarians are when you conduct research. In this age of technology, you can access most library resources from locations outside the library building. This is convenient, but students can easily forget or sometimes are not even aware that a librarian is available to them at their university library. This person is knowledgeable about the most efficient ways to use the tools provided by their library and how to access and use catalogs such as the *Mental Measurements Yearbook*. In my experience, librarians are eager to help and usually will spend extra time with students trying to dig deeper or be thorough with their research. When consulting with a librarian, it is important to do some basic research first and approach the librarian with a specific question. For example, do not ask, "What do you think is the best instrument to measure happiness?" Instead, follow all the steps described earlier. If you hit a roadblock, it is a good time to reach out to the librarian. Perhaps you found the link to the *Mental Measurements Yearbook* but cannot get it to open. Perhaps you entered a term into the search box of the yearbook, but you are having trouble interpreting the results.

In addition, learn how to use your library's interlibrary loan system. Although your library most likely will not have every article readily available, most libraries can order a copy of the article you need. Every library has a different system for submitting interlibrary loan requests, so see your librarian to find out how to order articles that are not in your university's library holdings. This is important. You should be able to get a copy of every article you need within a week or two of requesting it.

Faculty Advisor

Once you have the information about what instruments are available, share it with your advisor. Some good questions to ask your advisor are, Have I conducted a complete and thorough search for the instruments? Are you familiar with any of these instruments? Do you have a preference for the instruments I use? If so, why? What other information do you need about these instruments to help guide me toward choosing the best one for this study? If there are other experts consulting on your project, ask them the same questions.

The next chapter builds on the idea of gathering information about available instruments. I go over the specific types of information you need to know about each instrument, why it is important, and how to record and organize that information so you can easily refer back to it as you develop the method for your study.

SUMMARY

There are many tools available to help you identify instruments that measure the constructs you aim to study. At this stage of designing your study, your goal is to generate a comprehensive list of all potential instruments available for your study, so use every tool you can. Library databases and search engines can help you search for instruments using search terms or author names. Some books provide comprehensive lists of instruments, and other books and book chapters report information about instruments to measure specific constructs such as depression or categories of constructs such as school-based instruments. Empirical articles on the topic you are studying will report the instruments that were used in those studies. Librarians and faculty advisors may have some additional information for you as well.

4

Gathering and Organizing Information About Instruments

Y ou are now still in the information-gathering phase of instrument selection. Chapter 3 guided you through how to identify what instruments are available. Now that you have a list of those instruments, it is important to gather some details about each instrument so that you can compare and contrast the instruments. In this chapter, I explain what details you have to know, why each detail is important, and how to record this information in an organized system. Although it may seem tedious to take notes on multiple instruments you decide not to use, these notes will come in handy later when you prepare the study proposal for your advisor and others who will review and approve your study. At that stage, you will have to explain why you chose certain instruments and not others. Chapter 8 explains in depth how to write these descriptions. For now, just know that taking notes is important because you will rely on these notes later.

http://dx.doi.org/10.1037/0000192-005
Selecting and Describing Your Research Instruments, by K. S. McClure

GATHERING INFORMATION

The information you collect on each instrument will come from the articles, books, and chapters you found while conducting the searches that were discussed in Chapter 3. Sometimes, though, you will not be able to find some of the information you want. If you find yourself in that situation, you can also consult with experts who have published articles or instruments on the topics you wish to study. For example, you could email an author you identified in your backward author search if you have a particular question for which you cannot find the answer. You may find an instrument that appears to have good content and construct validity, but when you searched for data on the instrument's reliability, you could not find any. If you looked everywhere and are out of ideas, you could e-mail the instrument author to ask whether there are any published reliability data. Figure 4.1 is an example of an email you may send to the author.

MULTICULTURAL CONSIDERATIONS

The American Psychological Association published *Multicultural Guidelines: An Ecological Approach to Context, Identity, and Intersectionality* (2017b), which provides a framework and 10 guidelines for providing

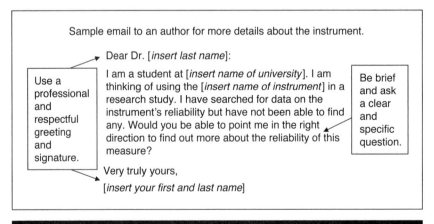

Figure 4.1

Sample email to an author for more details about the instrument.

multiculturally competent psychological services, including culturally appropriate and informed research. The multicultural guidelines state that researchers must attend to how research methodology, including instrumentation, is potentially shaped by the researchers' worldviews and assumptions. Furthermore, the document states, "testing and development of measures in different languages and among diverse cultures is critical to the development of . . . measures with culturally sound psychometric findings" (p. 64).

As researchers, we must also ensure that research samples are representative of the diverse populations we intend to study. Remember that *populations* are the entire group of people to whom the results of a study are intended to generalize. A *sample* is a subset of a population that is included in a study to draw conclusions about the population. When selecting instruments, be sure to consider the potential barriers that particular instruments may impose. These may include limitations related to reading, vision, cognitive or physical abilities, language spoken, or other considerations. Consider these issues as you gather the information described in this chapter.

INFORMATION TO GATHER

Purpose

Psychological instruments are created for a few different purposes. The two main purposes are for research or clinical assessment. You may be asking yourself whether there is a difference between a research instrument and a clinical assessment instrument or tool. There is, but it is sometimes difficult to see. For example, the Beck Depression Inventory-II (Beck, Steer, & Brown, 1996) can be used for both research and clinical purposes. Some instruments, however, have only been used and validated for research or clinical purposes, but not for both. It is your responsibility to find out whether there is research to support the research applicability of the instrument you select for your research study.

Why is the purpose of an instrument important to know? When selecting instruments for your research study, it is important to know whether the instrument has already been used for research purposes. If it has not been used for research purposes, you can still use it in your research. However, you will have to explain why it is the best instrument to use and that there are no other instruments available to you that have already been used in research. You may also have to conduct some additional analyses of the instrument's validity and reliability as part of your study to be confident that you are measuring what you intend to measure.

Scoring

It is essential to know how an instrument is scored before selecting a research instrument. Each instrument has a scoring method. Some use simple methods, such as calculating the sum of the score for each item. Others have complex scoring methods that include different weights for different items, and some use a technique called *reverse scoring*, where responses are recoded to reflect the opposite number from what the participant selected. This is done when items are written with positive as well as negative wording. Also, some scores are categorical, and some are continuous.

Sometimes different statistical analyses are required for categorical and continuous data. If your hypothesis assumes that the variable in your study is categorical, you will have to ensure that the instrument you use can provide scores that divide the variable into categories. Likewise, if your hypothesis assumes that the variable in the present study is continuous, your instrument score will have to provide continuous data.

Format

The format of an instrument is the way in which it is administered, as well as its language. As discussed in Chapter 2, one type of format is self-report. Self-report instruments can be further broken down into paper-and-pencil and computerized formats. Researchers should carefully consider the formats of the instruments that they include in their studies because the format can impact the diversity of the study sample. Some individuals prefer or have easier access to particular instrument formats. For example, I conduct some research with adults who have been diagnosed with cancer. Their ages can range from early 30s to late 80s. I find that, in general, the younger participants prefer to complete self-report questionnaires in a computer format online, whereas older participants prefer to complete the questionnaires in paper-and-pencil format. Whenever possible, I offer the participants the choice of online or paper-and-pencil format.

When considering instrument formats, try to choose formats that remove as many barriers as possible. Not only will this increase the size of the sample in your study but it will also increase the likelihood of having the most diverse sample of participants possible.

Languages

You may find some research instruments that are produced in several languages. The description of the languages in which the instruments are available is usually included in the library database records. There are several important issues to consider when choosing what language(s) to use for research instruments. The first consideration is the population you wish to study. Remember that the population is the group that you wish to understand or, in other words, the group to whom your results should generalize. The sample is the subset of the population that a researcher includes in his or her study. The sample should be a good representation of the population. Therefore, if the population speaks English, it is best to administer the instruments in English. However, if the population's primary language is Spanish, with limited or variable ability to read and understand English, and the instruments are administered in English, the validity of the instruments may be threatened due to the participants' lack of understanding of the instruments.

What happens if the instrument is only available in one language—let us say English—but the population speaks a different language? In this instance, the researcher may have to have the instrument professionally translated into the other language. It is important that the researcher does not try to translate the instrument without professional assistance. The validity and reliability of the translated instrument will have to be tested as well. *Back translation*, translating the questionnaire into another language and then having another translator translate it back into the original language, is the most thorough method of ensuring the translation is accurate and comparable between both language versions of the instrument.

What happens when the primary language of the population is varied, when different groups in the population have different primary languages? In this situation, it may be possible to administer the instrument in the participants' language of choice, as long as a professional translation is available. However, after collecting the data, it will be essential for the researchers to compare the personal information of the subgroups of participants to ensure that the groups do not systematically vary by individual characteristics such as age or by the language of the instrument because these could potentially threaten the validity of the study. If the groups do systematically vary by language of the instrument, consult with your research advisor on how to address this.

Accessibility

It is helpful to note anything about the instrument that makes it more accessible to all people. For example, note whether a self-report instrument is written for a particular reading level, whether a computerized test has a color-blind mode, and so forth. Also, note whether questions are written to account for other experiences that commonly co-occur in the population. For example, depression is an experience that can have physical symptoms, and it is common for older adults to have some physical ailments that are not related to depression. Some instruments that measure depression are specifically designed for older adults and do not place a heavy emphasis on physical symptoms.

Reliability

In Chapter 2, I reviewed the definitions of the various types of reliability. Information regarding internal reliability (typically reported in a statistical term called Cronbach's alpha or α) is usually the easiest to find. When selecting your instruments, you will use the internal reliability found in other studies to determine whether the instrument is internally reliable. When you complete your study, you will report the internal reliability of the instrument in your study. In addition to the internal reliability, look for and record information related to test–retest and alternate-forms reliability. Also, record the references in which you found the reliability information so you can go back to them later as needed. You can also keep these notes in Figure 4.2 with your notes on reliability.

Validity

Similarly, you should find and record information about the validity of the instruments. When gathering information about potential instruments to use, it is important to create notes for every type of validity that has been tested for every instrument you are considering. Figure 4.2 can help you keep these notes. It is likely that you will have to gather this information from multiple sources and that it will not be readily available to you in one article. Your notes should include the sources where you found the validity data.

Samples

You should also collect information about the samples that were studied using this instrument. When you use an instrument that has already been used in the sample you intend to study, you can compare your results with the other findings more easily.

Commercially Available or Public Domain Instruments

I discuss this issue in detail in Chapter 5, but it is worth mentioning briefly here as well. Some instruments are published by commercial publishers. Researchers who wish to use commercially published instruments must purchase them through the publisher and obtain permission to use them. This is similar to music companies owning and selling the rights to the

Possible Instruments Note-Taking Worksheet

Variable name: _____

Measure 1
  Title:
  Purpose:
  Scoring:
  Format(s):
  Language(s):
  Accessibility:
  Other considerations for individual differences and diversity:
  Validity:
    Construct
    Content
    Concurrent
    Predictive
  Reliability:
    Internal consistency
    Test–retest
    Alternate forms
  Samples with which it has been used:
  Ethical considerations:
  Ownership (commercial/author/public domain):
  References:

Measure 2
  Title:
  Purpose:
  Scoring:
  Format(s):
  Language(s):
  Accessibility:
  Other considerations for individual differences and diversity:
  Validity:
    Construct
    Content
    Concurrent
    Predictive
  Reliability:
    Internal consistency
    Test–retest
    Alternate forms
  Samples with which it has been used:
  Ethical considerations:
  Ownership (commercial/author/public domain):
  References:

Figure 4.2

Possible instruments note-taking worksheet.

songs that we purchase the right to download and play on our listening devices. Instruments developed with government-sponsored funding are often free and available to the public. For example, instruments developed in the United States with funding from the government (e.g., a grant from the National Institutes of Health) are available for researchers to use without charge. These are called instruments in the public domain, and researchers do not have to pay or obtain permission to use them. However, researchers do have to be qualified to use the instruments, an issue that is addressed in Chapter 7. In addition to commercially published instruments and those in the public domain, some instruments are developed by researchers without public grant funding and are not commercially published. If you would like to use one of these instruments, you must contact the researcher to ask for permission. Contact information for authors is reported in every journal article.

How do you know whether an instrument is commercially published, in the public domain, or owned by the author? See Chapter 5 for a more detailed discussion about this. Sometimes this information is easy to find, and sometimes it is not. First, look in the library databases. If you cannot find the information there, look in the primary source for the instrument. If you still cannot find the information, try searching the Internet. If you still cannot find how the instrument is published, e-mail the instrument author.

ORGANIZING AND TAKING GOOD NOTES

By now, I hope you agree that selecting instruments for your study is an important step in the process of research design. One of the pitfalls of this step, however, is that it sometimes does not feel important. Understandably, researchers, and especially new researchers, are eager to begin collecting the data and finding out the final results. Unfortunately, this eagerness can lead to sloppy record keeping in the middle of the study if you are not careful. Staying organized and taking good notes while selecting your instruments will save you a lot of time and will also help you quickly make adjustments if your first efforts to select an instrument do not work out. It is important to plan your organizational strategy first before you review each instrument and take notes. Next, I describe the steps you can take to get organized.

Set Up a Note-Taking Format

First, you have to choose how you will record the information. I recommend using a note-taking template such as the one in Figure 4.2.

Organize the Articles

It will also be helpful to organize the articles in a way that will help you find them later. I create electronic files for each measure. Then, when I read articles that used a particular measure, I store the article in the measure subfolder.

Naming Conventions

Set up a clear and consistent system for naming your electronic files. This system is called a *naming convention*. For example, when I wrote this book, I saved the file as Concise_Guide_Instruments. However, I saved a new copy of the book every time I edited it. This way, I had the old copy in case I made a mistake and accidentally deleted something or in case I wanted to look at an old draft. To keep track of the drafts, I added the date to the end of the name of each version (e.g., Concise_Guide_ Instruments_5_29_19). When I use the same naming convention, my electronic files are stored in order, and I can easily find the most up-to-date version of the document.

Back It Up

I have to confess that I am the worst at backing up my files. I think it is because I do not like to stop what I am doing. I have a bad habit of working right up to the last minute (or maybe even a few minutes longer) and then quickly logging out of my files. I do not recommend this at all, but I share it because I think it is quite common. Once we get a research "flow" going, it is hard to stop. That is why it is important to set up a plan for how and when to back up your files regularly and to follow through with that plan. Do not rely on the cloud to store your information. Computers and systems crash. You are spending hours collecting this information, so keep it safe, and keep an extra copy. I recommend backing up your files once a week. Always work from your main file and then store a backup file somewhere else. For example, if your main files are on Google Drive so that you can access it anywhere, download the files to the hard drive of your computer once a week and store them in a folder called *backup*. You can replace the old backup files with the new ones each week.

SUMMARY

After you have the comprehensive list of instruments you developed in the previous chapter, you have to gather detailed information about each instrument on your list. This chapter focused on the importance of taking clear and organized notes about specific characteristics of each possible instrument. Soon you will evaluate the strengths and weaknesses of these characteristics and use the information to make final decisions about which instruments to use in your study. At that point, you should refer back to the notes you kept as you worked through this chapter, so using consistent and organized notes will be helpful.

5

Permissions and Feasibility

You are almost ready to select the instruments you will use, but there are two more important considerations: (a) how to obtain permission to use the instruments and (b) whether to pilot the instruments for your specific study. I placed this chapter here for two reasons. First, you may come across information about how to obtain permission to use the instruments while you are collecting the other information about the instruments I discussed in Chapter 4 and you recorded in Figure 4.2. Second, obtaining permission to use an instrument may take time or be expensive. In some instances, you may find that the costs of obtaining permission to use a particular instrument will weigh into the decision-making process I describe in the next chapter. Therefore, it is important that you have this information early and before you proceed to Chapter 6. Also, some programs require students to demonstrate that

http://dx.doi.org/10.1037/0000192-006
Selecting and Describing Your Research Instruments, by K. S. McClure

they have permission to use their proposed instruments before their study proposals can be approved.

OBTAINING PERMISSION

First, I discuss obtaining permission to use the instruments. In this section, I describe how to identify who owns the rights to an instrument and how you can request permission to use the instrument. It is not uncommon for students to feel intimidated about contacting the author of an instrument or feel unsure about what to say, so I also provide an email template you can modify and use when seeking the appropriate permissions for your study.

Psychological and social science instruments are intellectual property, which means that someone owns the rights to those instruments, and researchers who use those instruments must do two things: (a) receive permission to use them and (b) cite the references to the instruments in their research proposals and manuscripts. In fact, obtaining permission to use research instruments is an action you can take to ensure that your study adheres to the ethical guidelines of psychology and other social science professions. In Chapter 7, I discuss more about the ethical guidelines of the American Psychological Association as they relate to research instruments.

For now, though, there are a few things you need to know about how instruments are made available and how to seek permission to use them. First, just because you can get a copy of an instrument does not mean you are automatically allowed to use it. Research instruments fall into three general categories of ownership. The first is those that are commercially published, which means that the instruments are owned by companies that must give permission for their use and usually charge a fee. The second category is those that are owned by the author. These instruments are typically published in journals either partially or in their entirety, but you still need permission from the authors to use them even if there is no cost. The third category is those that are in the public domain, which means that they are free and available to the public without any permissions required. In the next sections, I describe all these categories in more detail.

Commercially Published Instruments

As I mentioned, commercially published instruments are owned and sold by corporations. Corporations that sell psychology research instruments include MultiHealth Systems and Pearson. If you would like to use an instrument that is owned and distributed through one of these corporations, you have to place an order through that corporation. If you need assistance you can also contact the customer service department of most corporations and speak to a sales representative. The information about how to connect with a representative will be on the corporation's website.

When purchasing commercially published instruments, you have to fill out a form describing your research aims, hypotheses, and measures. If you are a student, you will most likely also have to have this form signed by your research advisor. Be sure to ask for a student discount. Many of these corporations offer a discounted price for students. Keep in mind that the application for the student discount will require your faculty advisor's signature, and it may take a few weeks for the corporation to process your request, so plan for this in the timeline for your study. Psychologists are happy to help student researchers, but they are not happy to receive requests to rush a job.

Timing when to obtain permission to use an instrument from a commercial publisher can be tricky. You have to present some information to your advisor and institutional review board (IRB) to show that you will likely be able to use the instrument, and you have to know how much it will cost. However, you should avoid incurring those costs until after your study is approved. I recommend discussing this timing with your advisor. Usually, you can present a copy of the instrument and pricing information to your advisor and IRB and then wait until after their approval before purchasing the rights to use the instruments.

Instruments Owned by the Author

Instruments owned by the author were developed by an individual or group of researchers. If you would like to use instruments owned by authors, you have to contact the first author of the instrument and ask for permission. The first author is the author whose name is listed first in the list of authors on the paper that first published a description of the instrument. Permission from authors is typically requested by email. Most instruments owned by the author are published in a journal article, and the contact author's email address is listed on the bottom of the first page of the manuscript or near the abstract. Use this email address to contact the author of the instrument. Explain your aims and hypotheses and that you would like to use their instrument. Most researchers are happy to have their instrument used, so feel free to contact them. Just make sure your communication is professional and brief and clearly states what you are requesting. Figure 5.1 provides an email template for requesting permission to use an instrument either when the instrument is available from the author or when you cannot figure out where to obtain permission for its use.

When granting permission to use their instruments, authors may ask you for more information about your study, or they may offer permission to use the instrument with the condition that you send them your final manuscript so that they are aware of the results of all the studies conducted with their instrument. If this is requested, make a note to yourself to do this, and be sure to send the final results to the instrument author. After all, the instrument author shared their work with you, so it

---

Dear Dr. (insert last name here):

I am a student at (*insert name of university*). I am designing a study on (*insert name of the general topic*) and my advisor's name is (*insert name of advisor*). The aim of the study is (*insert the study aim here*) and the hypotheses are (*insert the hypotheses here*). My advisor and I have discussed the possibility of using the (*insert name of the instrument*) to measure (*insert name of construct*) in this study. We plan to seek IRB approval to conduct the study soon. May I have your permission to use this instrument in my study? If you are not in the position of granting permission to use this instrument, will you kindly let me know who I should contact? I am sure you are very busy, and I appreciate you taking the time to consider my questions.

Sincerely,

(*insert your first and last name*)

Figure 5.1

Email template for requesting permission to use an instrument.

is only fair that you share yours as well. This is also a great way to build your professional network.

Public Domain Instruments

Some instruments are in the public domain, which means that they are free and available to the public. These instruments are often published in an article or on the Internet, and researchers can copy or download them and use them. Instruments in the public domain are typically the cheapest (free!) and easiest to access. Sometimes it is difficult to know when an instrument is in the public domain. If the article in which the instrument is published indicates that the instrument is in the public domain, you can trust that it is free to use without additional permission. Sometimes there are websites for instruments in the public domain. For example, the Center for Epidemiological Studies Depression Scale (CESD; Radloff, 1977) was originally developed to measure the prevalence and incidence of depression in the U.S. population. Researchers can download a copy of the most recent revision, the CESD-R, from https://www.cesd-r.com. Information about this instrument, including a statement that the instrument is in the public domain and free to use, is also available on this website.

If you are not sure whether an instrument is in the public domain, you should ask your advisor. After consulting with your advisor, you may decide together that it is appropriate for you to send an e-mail, such as the one in Figure 5.1, to the author of the instrument.

Next, I discuss testing out the instruments, a process called *piloting*. The purpose of piloting the instruments is to make sure they will work well in your study. The rest of this chapter describes the importance of piloting the instruments, as well as suggestions for how and when to pilot and what information to collect.

FEASIBILITY

Feasibility refers to ease or convenience. To determine the feasibility of an instrument, you will have to consider how easy and convenient it will be for the sample in your study to complete the instrument, as well as how easy or convenient it will be for you to administer it. This is not always easy to predict, so gathering some preliminary information before collecting the data for your study may be helpful.

A *pilot study* is a practice study that allows researchers to collect information about how the study design works. Many researchers conduct pilot studies to test how well the manipulations in their experiments work. Although you and your advisor may decide that such a pilot study is needed for your experiment, this is beyond the scope of this book on instrument selection. However, one small part of a pilot study may include piloting the instruments. This section of this chapter focuses on piloting the instruments you will use to measure variables in your studies.

What else do you have to know about these instruments? You have done so much research on them already. It is important to try them out with the types of people and in the setting that you wish to use in your study. You can do this by simply asking a few people who are similar to the people you want to have in your study to fill out the measures and collecting some information about their experience using the instruments. Then it is up to you which questions you ask. Look at the notes you took on language and accessibility in Figure 4.2 and ask about those issues to make sure that participants could complete your instruments fully and accurately. You may wish to ask whether the instruments were difficult to read or upsetting. Read the articles about the instruments to see whether anything is mentioned about why people did not complete other studies using these instruments and ask about those issues as well. Finally, consult with your faculty advisor and colleagues about other issues to check when piloting the instruments.

Keep in mind that when you are piloting your instruments, although it is not your main study, the process still includes volunteer participants. Chapter 7 discusses research ethics as they relate to instrument selection. Part of this includes obtaining permission from an IRB to ensure that research is conducted ethically with minimal harm to the participants. The IRB will review and approve your process for piloting the instruments, as well as your main study, so do not conduct a pilot study on your instruments before you read Chapter 7 or, more important, before you have permission from your institution's IRB. Then, after you have the feedback from your pilot study, you can plan how to make modifications based on the feedback. Be sure to consult your advisor.

SUMMARY

Gathering permission to use the instruments, as well as information about their feasibility in your specific study, may require some additional work beyond looking up information in databases and search engines, books and book chapters, or articles. You have to understand who owns each instrument and secure information from that owner. Once you have permission from the owner, and possibly also from the IRB, you may also have to test out the instrument in a pilot study to gather some information about how easy or convenient the instrument is to use.

6

Using the Evidence to Guide Your Instrument Selection

Now that you have information about possible instruments you may use in your psychological or social science research study, it is time to choose the best one. A good rule of thumb is to choose the easiest and quickest instrument that can validly and reliably measure the construct you are trying to measure. However, there are also some important factors to consider. You have to consider what resources you have available to acquire and use the instruments and whether the instruments are a good fit with the methodology of your study. In this chapter, I discuss these factors and describe a process for weighing the benefits and drawbacks of each instrument. The previous chapter provided detailed instructions about how to contact instrument publishers, which is an essential step before finalizing any decisions about instruments.

http://dx.doi.org/10.1037/0000192-007
Selecting and Describing Your Research Instruments, by K. S. McClure

KNOW YOUR RESOURCES

The resources available to conduct a study have a large impact on the instruments that are selected. The most important resources to consider are money and time. Let us begin with cost. As you now know from the information you gathered, the cost of instruments can vary greatly. When calculating costs, consider the cost per administration. For example, if you aim to collect data from a sample of 100 participants, and the instrument you prefer costs $1.00 per administration, you will need $100.00 plus tax, a shipping charge, and possibly a flat fee for the instrument manual as well. An *instrument manual* is a document describing the main characteristics of a psychological instrument, such as the structure, scoring and interpretation, and psychometric properties. Some instruments have manuals, and others do not. If you plan to use an instrument that has a manual to accompany it, you should acquire the manual. When instruments are free, remember to calculate printing costs if you plan to duplicate the instrument and administer it using paper and pencil. Another option for administering self-report instruments is through data collection software such as Survey Monkey or Qualtrics. Keep in mind that you will need permission from the instrument developers to administer the instrument in an online format. Sometimes the instrument developers charge a fee for permission to administer the instrument online. Some software has a cost as well.

Now let us move on to the resource of time. There are three things to consider: the time the participants have to complete the instruments, the time you and your team have to score the instruments and enter the data, and the time you have to complete the entire study. Participants in psychology or social science research studies are wonderful. They give their time to do all sorts of things in the name of science, and they usually do it for free or for a small reward. I have found that potential participants also have the best intentions to complete our studies. However, life gets in the way. Just like the rest of us, they have busy schedules, they multitask, and they cannot do everything they want to do. When selecting an instrument, try to choose one that your intended sample is likely to have the time and motivation to complete. You can choose the perfect instrument to measure the construct in your study, but if the participants do not complete it, you have not measured anything at all.

Your time is valuable too. Keep that in mind when considering how long it takes to reproduce and score an instrument. Is the scoring difficult? Is it cumbersome? Maybe it is worth it if the instrument is effective at measuring the construct. But make sure you budget enough time or secure enough assistants to complete the scoring. Finally, you may have a specific time frame to complete your study. Perhaps you have one semester or one year. Keep this in mind when you select your instruments. Some instruments may take a long time to administer and score and may make it difficult for you to keep to your timeline.

REVIEW YOUR AIMS

It is always a good idea to stop and review the aims of your study at each step of developing the research design. Even though it is quite possible that a review of your aims may not change the instruments you select, it is helpful to stay focused on why you are conducting the study and what you intend to understand better after the study is complete.

CONSIDER THE INTENDED SAMPLE

I already discussed the need to consider how much time people will have to participate in your study. There are a few other things to consider. First, was this instrument designed to be used with the group of people you plan to study? If you are studying a general group of healthy White adults with average reading abilities who see and hear well, there is a good chance that several of the instruments on your list have been used with your intended sample. However, if the population you are studying is more specific—adolescents, Latina women, adults with cancer, for example—it is helpful to choose an instrument that has already been used with similar types of people. You will have more confidence that the instrument will also be valid and reliable in your study, and you will be able to compare the results of your study with results from other studies of similar groups of people more easily. You will be more interested in comparing the conclusions of your study with other studies about similar people than with studies about people that have nothing in common with the people you are studying.

CONSIDER THE BENEFITS AND DRAWBACKS OF USING MORE THAN ONE INSTRUMENT

Perhaps after looking at the instruments on your list, you discovered that there is not one instrument that perfectly measures the construct you want to study. New researchers are often surprised to learn that most research instruments are imperfect. We social scientists do our best to measure abstract concepts, but it is not a perfect process, so we rely on patterns and parsimony to make our conclusions. Researchers have to choose the best instrument they can for each study, and over time, our collection of studies helps us understand people and the world in which we live. You do have the option, though, of using more than one instrument to measure the same construct in one study. The benefit of using more than one instrument is that when the measurements gathered from both instruments are correlated, you have more confidence in your findings. For example, I was once part of a research team that used two instruments to measure depression (Nezu, Nezu, Felgoise, McClure, & Houts, 2003)— a self-report instrument called the Profile of Mood States (McNair, Lorr, & Droppleman, 1992) and a semistructured interview called the Hamilton Rating Scale for Depression (Hamilton, 1960). We analyzed the data twice—once with each instrument—and the results were comparable with both analyses. The drawbacks of using more than one instrument are that it takes more time and money to administer the instruments and to analyze the data more than once. It is hard to say whether it would be a drawback or a strength of the study if the results do not come out the same in the analyses with the different measures. On the one hand, it would be a drawback because you would not have as much confidence in your findings. On the other hand, it could also be a strength because the results provide new information about the measures of the constructs that you are studying.

INSTRUMENT DECISION-MAKING NEXT STEPS

At this point, I like to use a simple ✔ strategy. Make a column for each characteristic that is important to your study and then add a ✔ to note that this instrument does it well. Most of the time, you should choose the instrument that has the most ✔s. However, when you see all the strengths and weaknesses laid out in one place, you may discover that certain strengths are more important to your study or that there are certain weaknesses you cannot live with at all. Then you will choose the instrument for your study, feeling confident that you have weighed all the options and made the best decision. You can use Figure 6.1 as a guide. Feel free to add or delete columns as you see fit. Even though this decision-making process might sound painfully tedious, I think you will discover that it is quick and painless.

You thought you were finished, but there are a few more steps. It is time to consult with experts again, starting with your advisor. Bring Figure 6.1 to your next advising meeting and go over it. Then, of course, check off the corresponding item in your Advisor Consultation Checklist (Figure 1). After you get approval from your faculty advisor, consult

Decision-Making Worksheet

You can use this table to compare and contrast the strengths and weakness of each instrument. List the name of each instrument in the column on the left. Then place a ✔ in each column for which the instrument is satisfactory. Instrument with the most ✔ marks may be the best fit.

Variable name: _____

Instrument name	Does it fit the study aims?	Do I have the resources?	Will the sample use this well?	Does the format fit the method?
Instrument 1				
Instrument 2				
Instrument 3				

Figure 6.1

Decision-making worksheet.

with peers and experts in the field as well. Peers can be other student researchers in your class or on your team if you are working on a research team. Experts in the field may be academics familiar with the topic or professionals familiar with the target population. Figure 6.2 illustrates the decision-making process you will follow.

Aims and Hypotheses
Review the study aim or aims. Will the instrument help measure the variables listed in the study aim(s) and hypothesis or hypotheses?

Resources
What is my financial budget, and how much time do I have? Do I have the time and money to use this instrument? Will I be able to obtain permission to use the instrument?

Sample
Have other researchers successfully used this instrument with the population of interest in my study? Will the population of interest find this instrument to be understandable and user-friendly? Are there any special considerations for the population of interest (e.g., developmental needs, language, sensory considerations such as vision or hearing needs)?

Format
Is the format of this instrument compatible with the method that I selected? Will participants be able to complete the instrument? Will I be able to collect and store the data?

Multiple Measures
Is it possible for me to measure the construct with more than one instrument? Would it be beneficial? Is it practical? Do I have the resources?

Consultations
Have I consulted with my advisor, my peers, and experts to ensure that I am making the best decision?

Figure 6.2

Decision-making flow chart.

SUMMARY

Once you have armed yourself with the information about each instrument, the time will have arrived to use this information to decide which instruments to use. Decision-making checklists such as the one in Figure 6.1 may help you compare and contrast the characteristics of the instruments. The decision-making flow chart in Figure 6.2 provides a visual representation of this decision-making process.

7

Following Ethical Principles
and Guidelines

Researchers have a responsibility to ensure that their studies have a positive impact on science and, ultimately, on society. They also have a responsibility to ensure that their studies do not cause any harm. Fortunately, there are professional standards you can follow to ensure that the benefits of your study outweigh any risks and that you have avoided all unnecessary risks to participants. In this chapter, I describe institutional review boards (IRBs) that oversee the ethical conduct of researchers. I then describe the *Ethical Principles of Psychologists and Code of Conduct* published by the American Psychological Association (APA Ethics Code; 2017a) and specifically discuss which principles and standards in this code of conduct apply to instrument selection.

http://dx.doi.org/10.1037/0000192-008
Selecting and Describing Your Research Instruments, by K. S. McClure

INSTITUTIONAL REVIEW BOARDS

In most institutions, and especially colleges and universities, researchers must apply to and receive approval from an IRB before conducting research with human participants. IRBs are teams of professionals that institutions entrust to review research studies for adherence to the ethical principles of the profession. The most important role of the IRB is to ensure that researchers are making every effort to protect participants from potential harm. IRBs review the study proposals before data is collected. As part of the application process, they may also require that the researchers participate in ethics training (usually online).

You should consult with your advisor about whether you have to receive IRB approval to conduct your study. If you do, also consult with your advisor about where to find your institution's information about the application procedures. It is usually available online or in a learning management system such as Canvas or Blackboard. In general, all IRB applications request that you briefly state the study aims, hypotheses, and methods. Because they are charged with protecting participants, the IRB will require detailed information about exactly what each participant will be doing, including detailed information about the instruments you will ask the participants to complete.

The first time they complete an IRB application, many students are surprised by the level of detail IRBs require about the instruments in their studies. A good rule of thumb is to provide as many details as you can about what the participants will be doing, including what they are doing to complete the research instruments, so that the people who read your application can envision what will happen to the participants throughout your study. Therefore, when describing the instruments, you should describe the format (e.g., self-report questionnaire), method of administration (e.g., paper and pencil or online), and length of the instrument (number of questions and approximate amount of time needed to complete). You also must describe any risks the participant may take by completing the instruments. For example, if the questions are sensitive because they ask for information people may find personal or emotional, you must state that. Also, describe where the participants will complete the questionnaire and any steps you will take to ensure privacy while participants complete the instruments and in how you store the instrument data afterward. In Chapter 8, I provide more details about how to describe your instruments for the IRB, and I also provide an example for you to follow. Before you move on, though, let us discuss some of the ethical principles that IRBs consider and how they apply to research instrument selection.

CODE OF CONDUCT AND GUIDELINES

There are some important ethical considerations when selecting instruments for psychology and social science research. *Merriam-Webster* defines *ethics* (n.d.) as "the principles of conduct governing an individual or a group." Two documents describe specific rules of conduct related to psychology and social science research.

The APA Ethics Code is a comprehensive document that describes these rules of conduct for psychologists. The document includes the five general principles of beneficence and nonmaleficence, fidelity and responsibility, integrity, justice, and respect for people's rights and dignity. There are also 10 sections that explain how the principles apply to specific aspects of psychological work. Section 8, Research and Publication, specifies 15 ethical considerations that apply. Everyone conducting psychological or social science research should carefully read Section 8 of the APA Ethics Code.

The Belmont Report: Ethical Principles and Guidelines for the Protection of Human Subjects of Research (National Commission for the Protection of Human Subjects of Biomedical and Behavioral Research, 1979) is a document provided by the U.S. Department of Health and Human Services for the ethical conduct of biomedical and behavioral research involving human subjects. The Belmont Report includes the three principles of respect for persons, beneficence, and justice. The report also includes ethical principles that apply to psychology research and, more broadly, to other types of research that include human participants, whereas the APA Ethics Code is specific to psychology research.

The two documents are complementary. Psychology researchers should know about both documents. You should refer specifically to the APA Ethics Code when developing your studies.

ETHICAL PRINCIPLES

In this section, I discuss the five ethical principles: respect for persons, beneficence and nonmaleficence, justice, fidelity and responsibility, and integrity. I then also discuss how the principles apply to the instrument selection procedures in this book.

Respect for Rights and Dignity

The principle of respect for people's rights and dignity means that psychologists value the dignity and worth of all people. This includes the right to privacy, confidentiality, and self-determination (APA, 2017a). Researchers respect people's *privacy* by not intruding on their personal space without permission. For example, researchers do not enter people's homes or work settings unannounced or without permission, and they do not record individuals without their permission. *Confidentiality* means that when researchers have private information that individuals share through their participation in a study, the researchers keep it safe and do not share it with others. Researchers strictly follow this and do not even disclose whether an individual has participated in a study. For example, I was once on vacation, and I saw a celebrity. Later that day, I told my friends who I saw—what car she was driving, what she was wearing, and that she waved to me. In contrast, I was once working on a study, and a local celebrity was one of the participants. I wanted to tell my friends the same type of thing about this person, but because I was following the APA Ethics Code, I did not say a word about this research participant.

Self-determination is the right to make one's own decisions. In research, that means the right to choose to participate and to stop participating whenever one chooses and without consequence. Individuals also need information about the studies they are considering participating in, so there is a process called *informed consent*. This means that researchers provide information about the activities participants will engage in and the risks and benefits of participation before individuals agree to participate. Researchers provide complete and accurate information and do not deceive people about what will happen. There are some rare instances when keeping the true purpose of a study or using some deception is necessary to test a hypothesis. In these instances, the researchers must demonstrate that the benefits of the study outweigh the costs of not conducting the study, that participants will not be harmed, and that there is absolutely no other way to conduct the study without deception. Researchers must then tell the participants the truth after the study is completed and offer support for any consequences the deception may have caused.

When selecting instruments, it is important that you consider privacy, confidentiality, and self-determination. When selecting an instrument, ask yourself three things: (a) Would completing this instrument in view of other people compromise a participant's dignity, and, if so, is it possible for participants to complete this instrument in a private space? (b) Is it possible for me to keep the responses to this instrument confidential, and what would have to be done to ensure that confidentiality (e.g., use ID numbers instead of names on paper-and-pencil questionnaires, remove data from cloud storage in online data collection methods as quickly as possible)? and (c) How can participants stop completing an instrument if or when they wish to do so?

Beneficence and Nonmaleficence

The principles of *beneficence* and *nonmaleficence* mean that psychologists strive to do good and not to harm others. In measurement, this means that researchers ask questions in a sensitive way, using inclusive language and avoiding judgment or communication that would contribute to negative stereotypes or stigma. Under the principle of beneficence and nonmaleficence, researchers must also have the appropriate level of knowledge and training to administer and interpret the instrument. In psychology, student researchers usually have to be supervised by an experienced researcher when using psychological instruments to ensure that the student is using the instrument properly and is not scoring or interpreting the data incorrectly or in another way that could lead to inaccurate conclusions.

Justice

Justice means that all persons must have access to the benefits of psychological knowledge. In research, this means that researchers must attempt to select participants for a study in a way that ensures that all members of the target population have an equal chance of participating in the study. Some of this is impacted by sampling methods. However, the instruments used in a study may also affect who participates. Researchers should select instruments that are valid and accessible for all members of a population. Adaptations of instruments for persons with disabilities or in a variety of languages or formats should be considered and should be used whenever possible. For example, I often use self-report questionnaires in my research with adults with cancer. It is easiest for me to use a computer format because I can simply share a URL, and I can download the participant data right into my statistical analysis software. Paper-and-pencil formats are a lot more work for me because I have to make photocopies, collate, provide mail-in envelopes or collect the questionnaires in person, manually enter all of the data, and then check the data entry for errors. However, I always offer both formats (computer and paper-and-pencil) and allow participants to choose the format that suits them best. If I did not, my studies would exclude people who do not have computers or who are not comfortable using computerized questionnaires, and this could result in some systematic bias in the samples. I would not have confidence that my results would apply to people with less access to or comfort with computers.

Fidelity and Responsibility

The principle of *fidelity and responsibility* means that psychologists are expected to act responsibly and be honest. For example, researchers should not use instruments that they do not understand or are not qualified to use, student researchers should select and use instruments under the supervision of their research advisors, and researchers should not give clinical diagnoses if they are not also trained clinicians. In addition, researchers should understand and accurately communicate the psychometric properties of the instruments, communicate clearly when they adapt the instruments for any reason, and score and interpret the instruments accurately.

Integrity

There is one more ethical principle that applies to instruments, and that is integrity. *Integrity* means telling the truth and representing oneself accurately. I am sure you have already learned about plagiarism and how to give credit when citing others' work. It is also important to give credit for instrument developments. As I discussed in Chapter 5, you must reference the articles in which instruments are described and published, and you must receive permission from the owners of the instruments before you use them in your study.

SUMMARY

It is important that you consider ethical principles when selecting your instruments. It is likely that an IRB will have to review and approve your research design, including your instruments. Consult your faculty advisor about the IRB requirements at your institution. The APA Ethics Code can serve as a helpful guide for considering the ethics of your study. It is important that the instruments you use will not cause unnecessary discomfort or other types of harm, that participants are aware of what they are agreeing to do when they complete the instruments and that they know how to stop completing the instruments if they wish to discontinue the study, and that data from the instruments are stored in a way that protects participants' private information. In addition, it is important that the instruments are offered in a format that allows the sample to be a good representation of the population you wish to study. This may require you to offer multiple formats or modify formats to remove barriers related to language or accessibility. Finally, it is also important that you receive permission to use the instruments and credit the authors of the instruments when you cite their work.

8

Describing Instruments Effectively for Different Audiences

After you select your instruments, you have to write descriptions of them for a few different audiences. In this chapter, I address how to describe research instruments for three types of audiences: the audience for the final manuscript once the study is completed, advisors during a research proposal, and institutional review board (IRB). You will have different audiences as you develop your projects, and consideration of the audience is essential because the content of an instrument description will vary for different audiences. If you are having flashbacks to your grade school language arts teacher telling you that the audience is important, now is the perfect time to send that person some good vibes, so they know their lessons stuck with you. Writing for different audiences requires careful thought and attention. Even doctoral students writing their dissertations find it challenging to write a description of an instrument for different audiences the first time.

http://dx.doi.org/10.1037/0000192-009
Selecting and Describing Your Research Instruments, by K. S. McClure

Now that you have read about the instruments that measure the constructs of interest in your study, you know that there is a lot of information about them. As I discussed in Chapter 4, it is important that you have all this information and that you store it in an organized manner. However, you will not be describing all the information and, in fact, it is your job to select the most important information to communicate. Information about the construct being measured, instrument format, references to the original source or the validation study conducted to develop the instrument, and psychometric properties should be included in all descriptions of measures. Additional information will vary for each audience.

Next, I explain how to describe the instruments for each type of audience. Figures 8.1, 8.2, and 8.3 provide examples of each type of description. The examples are about the measurement of social problem solving and are taken from a study that one of my students conducted on social problem solving and posttraumatic growth in breast cancer survivors (Markman et al., 2019). The instrument was measuring the construct of social problem solving, a process that individuals use to discover ways of coping with problems that come up in their daily lives.

FINAL MANUSCRIPT AUDIENCE

Let us begin by discussing how to describe the instrument for your final manuscript audience. I begin here for two reasons: (a) This is the description you see most often because you also read instrument descriptions in manuscripts, and (b) although you will write this description last, the other two descriptions will be longer variations of this final description.

Many people may read your final manuscript if you publish it in your university's electronic archives or a professional journal. There are two good resources to guide what you should include in this section. The first is the *Publication Manual of the American Psychological Association* (American Psychological Association [APA], 2010). The second is Journal Article Reporting Standards for Quantitative Research in Psychology (JARS; Appelbaum et al., 2018). Appelbaum et al. (2018) provides detailed information about what to report about instruments in Table 1 (pp. 6–7). Specifically, see the Measures and Covariates, Quality of Measurements, Instrumentation, and Psychometrics subsections of the Method section of the table. This document requires that researchers define all measures, information on the psychometric properties, and estimates of the reliability of the instrument in the study. In other words, after you finish your study, you have to report information about the reliability of the measures in the study.

Figure 8.1 is an example of how to write a description of an instrument for the final manuscript. You can also use the other papers you read when you were gathering information about the instruments you selected as examples for how to write them up in a final manuscript. Be sure to keep in mind, though, that the JARS were updated in 2018, so studies published before then may not report all the information that is currently required. The JARS should be the ultimate guide for what to include in a description of your instruments, and Table 1 of Appelbaum et al. (2018) is a helpful tool to guide you. The description of each instrument should include (a) the format, (b) the purpose of instrument, (c) what the respondents (participants) do, (d) general statements about the psychometric properties with references to the original sources that reported the psychometric properties, (e) how the scores are calculated, and (f) how the scores are interpreted. This final detail about how the scores are interpreted will be important to the readers of your final manuscript. When they read the mean scores of the measures in the results section of your paper, they will want to know what those scores mean. At the most basic level, you should indicate what a high or low score means. If you are measuring variables related to clinical diagnoses such as depression or anxiety, there may also be clinical cutoffs available. *Clinical cutoffs* are ranges of scores that correspond to levels of mental health symptom severity or diagnoses. If you are studying a clinical population, report clinical cutoffs when they are available.

The section header is the name of the instrument.

Reference the articles where the instrument was published and where the psychometric data is reported.

Provide information about the psychometric properties (validity and reliability).

Social Problem-Solving Inventory, Revised: Short Form

The Social Problem-Solving Inventory, Revised: Short Form (SPSI-R:S) is a 25-item self-report questionnaire that measures a person's ability to solve problems and make effective decisions (D'Zurilla & Nezu, 1990; D'Zurilla, Nezu, & Maydeu-Olivares, 2002). It examines multiple facets of problem solving, including orientation and style processes. Items load onto factors within categories of problem orientation or problem-solving style. Within the problem orientation domain, subscales include positive and negative problem orientations. Within the problem-solving style domain, subscales include rational, impulsivity/careless, or avoidance problem-solving style. This measure demonstrates strong internal consistency ($\alpha = 0.69$–0.95 for each subscale) and test–retest reliability ($\alpha = 0.72$–0.91). The internal consistency of the SPSI subscales in this study were $\alpha = .77$ for positive problem orientation, $\alpha = .80$ for negative problem orientation, $\alpha = .83$ for rational problem solving, $\alpha = .70$ for impulsivity/careless style, and $\alpha = 0.81$ for AS.

Begin by describing the format of the instrument. For example, this one is self-report. Provide some details, such as how many items and how participants fill it out.

Be sure to report reliability data from your study.

Figure 8.1

Sample description of instrument final manuscript audience. This is the description of the measure printed in the final manuscript published in the *Journal of Clinical Psychology in Medical Settings*. From "Social Problem Solving and Posttraumatic Growth New Possibilities in Postoperative Breast Cancer Survivors," by E. S. Markman, K. S. McClure, C. E. McMahon, N. Zelikovsky, B. W. Macone, and A. J. Bullock, 2019, *Journal of Clinical Psychology in Medical Settings, 26,* pp. 1–9. Copyright 2019 by Springer Nature. Reprinted with permission.

ADVISOR AUDIENCE

Now let us go back and discuss how these descriptions may be different for audiences you will work with before writing the final manuscript. The first audience who will read about your proposed instruments is your advisor. Your advisor may be both a collaborator and a gatekeeper. In the collaborator role, your advisor will want to know as much as possible about these measures. As a gatekeeper, your advisor will want to know that all other options for measuring the construct were considered, the reasons why the selected instrument is the best instrument to use, and that any potential harm to participants will be minimized. Therefore, your job is to provide enough information to your advisor to allow them to collaborate with you, ensure that you are making a well-informed and logical decision, and that risk to participants will be minimal.

Describing the instruments to your advisor requires both simple description and critical thinking. Descriptions for your advisor about the instruments you plan to use should be in paragraph format and may be as long as one to two pages for each instrument that you plan to use. (In other words, if you are measuring two constructs using two separate instruments, you should write a three- to four-page description of both of these instruments.) You should write a separate section for each variable you are measuring. For example, the measures included in the figures of this chapter describe instruments measuring social problem solving, but the study my student conducted examined another construct called posttraumatic growth as well. The paper she wrote for her advisor (me) at the proposal stage of her study had one section describing instruments for social problem solving and another section describing instruments measuring posttraumatic growth. In each section, begin with a paragraph or two describing the variable you plan to measure. Provide a definition of the variable and references to the authors who defined it. If a variable has been defined more than one way, write a paragraph about each definition, again citing clear references for each definition. This is the simple description part of the task. Then write your own paragraph noting which definition you plan to use in your study and explaining why you arrived at this decision. Cite relevant papers to support your decision whenever you can. This is the critical thinking part of the task.

Next, briefly describe the instruments most commonly used to measure the variable as defined by the definition that you selected. Most of the time, you will find somewhere between one and five instruments that are commonly used to measure a particular variable. You can provide this information in a list. It would also be helpful to include a copy of the decision-making worksheet you developed in Figure 6.1 of Chapter 6 and refer your advisor to the worksheet for more information. Again, this is a simple description task. Then state which instrument you plan to use, explain why, and offer evidence to support your decision. This is another critical thinking task.

Once you have identified the instrument you plan to use, provide more details about the instrument. Always describe the format (e.g., paper-and-pencil, online), length (e.g., 20 questions), and how long it takes to complete. Next, note whether you will be using the entire instrument or just part of it. Some instruments have a total score and subscale scores for parts of the measure. Explain which score or scores you plan to use and why. Then provide information about each aspect of the measure that you researched in Chapter 4 and recorded in Figure 4.2. If you plan to use only part of the instrument, be sure to provide the validity and reliability data about that part of the instrument. For example, I often use the Social Problem-Solving Inventory–Revised (D'Zurilla, Nezu, & Maydeu-Olivares, 2002). This self-report instrument provides a total score and five subscale scores. If I only plan to use one subscale—for example, the Negative Problem Orientation subscale—in my study, I should provide information about the reliability and validity of the Negative Problem Orientation subscale. You do not have to include information about the reliability and validity of the other subscales if you do not plan to use them.

Students often wonder what level of detail to include about the validity and reliability of the measures. Another name for the information about reliability and validity is *psychometric properties*. Deciding which psychometric properties to report also requires some critical thinking, and this is an area for which you may want to consult with your advisor or collaborators for some advice. For some instruments, little is known about the psychometric properties. In those instances, it is best to make a note of that and report everything you found. Other instruments have been well developed and have decades of research on their psychometric properties. It would be impractical and not helpful to report all those data. In these instances, a good rule of thumb is to

For my student's study on social problem solving, I would provide the following information to my advisor.

Variable name: Social problem solving

Description of the variable: Social problem solving is the process individuals engage in to discover ways of coping with everyday problems (Nezu & Nezu, 2019).

Defining the variable: There are a few ways to define social problem solving. The definition I selected is consistent with the model described for emotion-centered problem-solving therapy (Nezu & Nezu, 2019). This model includes five aspects of social problem solving.

Main measures: The instruments most commonly used to measure social problem solving are the Social Problem-Solving Inventory–Revised: Short Form (D'Zurilla, Nezu, & Maydeu-Olivares, 2002), Problem Solving Inventory (Heppner & Petersen, 1982), and the Means-End Problem Solving Procedures (Platt & Spivack, 1975). I selected the Social Problem-Solving Inventory–Revised: Short Form because it measures the five subscales of social problem solving in Nezu and Nezu's (2019) model. In addition, it has been used with samples of adult cancer patients (Nezu, Nezu, Felgoise, McClure, & Houts, 2003).

Figure 8.2

Sample description of instrument advisor audience. In addition to the information above, provide all the information in Figure 8.1 for your advisor, as well. However, you will not be able to provide the reliability data for your study until after you collect the data.

(a) report the psychometric properties from a review article about the instrument, if one is available; (b) report the psychometric properties that were measured in a sample most similar to the one you aim to study; and (c) report any controversy about the instrument or weaknesses in the psychometric properties that may have been identified in other studies. Figure 8.2 is an example of how to write a description of an instrument for your advisor.

INSTITUTIONAL REVIEW BOARD AUDIENCE

Finally, let us discuss the one additional audience reading about your instruments—the IRB. After your advisor approves the method of your study, which will include the instruments, you will submit an application to the IRB for approval to conduct your study. As mentioned in

the preceding chapter on ethics, the IRB monitors studies that are conducted with human participants to ensure that the studies are following
good ethical principles and that no one is being harmed by the research.
Some studies with minimal risk are reviewed by only one person on the
IRB. Other studies that involve more contact with participants and higher
risk are reviewed by a team of professionals (often three to five people).
It will be helpful for you to be aware that the people on an IRB are usually
interprofessional, which means that they represent a variety of fields or
disciplines. It is possible that the board reviewing your study will not have
any psychologists on it at all. It is always good practice to avoid jargon
in your writing as much as possible, and it is especially important when
writing an IRB application that will be read by individuals who may not
be familiar with the jargon and technical terms of psychology. Chapter 3 of the *Publication Manual of the American Psychological Association*
is a great resource for improving the continuity, flow, conciseness, and
clarity of your writing. I highly recommend reviewing it before you write
an IRB application.

Keeping in mind that the IRB's job is to minimize risks to participants, think about what details about the instruments are most important for the IRB to know. It is essential that you inform the IRB of any
risks participants may experience as a result of completing the instruments in your study. For example, if you are asking about trauma with a
sample of folks who have experienced trauma, you should explain what
risks the participants may experience during or after reading and answering questions about their trauma. If the risks are minimal because the
questions are not sensitive and the sample in your study is not vulner-
able, you should state that too. In addition to wanting to know about the
risks the instruments may pose, the IRB will also want to know about
the format and length of the instruments to help the IRB understand
what the participants will do. If you plan to use survey instruments, the
survey questions are also important so the IRB knows how intrusive or
sensitive the questions are. Moreover, the IRB will be reassured if you
can cite other studies that have used the same measures. Finally, the IRB

will be interested in the basic psychometric properties of the instruments because they will want to know that the instruments are likely to provide a valid and reliable measure of your constructs and, therefore, will not be a waste of the participants' time. Although it is not the job of the IRB to evaluate the potential contributions of your study to the field, you do have to demonstrate that the risk to the participants, however minimal it may be, will have the potential to make a contribution to science. Figure 8.3 is an example of how to write a description of an instrument for the IRB.

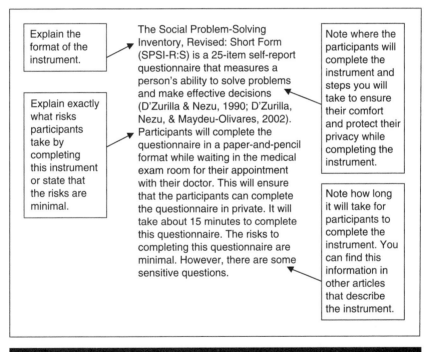

Figure 8.3

Sample description of instrument institutional review board audience. For the institutional review board, provide all the information in Figure 8.1, except the reliability data for your study, which you will not have until after you collect the data. In addition, provide information about what the instrument will require the participants to do and what risks the participants will take by completing the instrument.

SUMMARY

You will describe your instruments to three main audiences as you go through the process of conducting your research study. First, you will describe your instruments to your faculty advisor, who will approve your instrument selection. Next, you will describe your instruments to the members of the IRB, who will approve the ethics of your research design. Finally, you will describe your instruments for other researchers who read the final manuscript describing your entire study, including the results and conclusions. Some information will be the same for each audience, and some information will be tailored to the specific needs of the readers. This chapter explained what each audience will be considering and provided examples of descriptions for each audience.

9

Troubleshooting

Even the most prepared researchers run into barriers selecting research instruments. Do you remember the analogy at the beginning of this book about the musician selecting the right guitar for the right song, venue, and audience? Sometimes the perfect guitar does not exist for a particular situation. Other times the perfect guitar is out there, but it is too expensive, and the musician cannot afford it. Sometimes the guitar string breaks midway through a song, and the musician has to use another, less perfect guitar. The song is still played. The musician and audience know that the "perfect" song does not exist, and the song will be played again another time in a different place and with a different instrument. In the same way, the perfect research instrument does not exist. In social science, we do our best to observe and describe abstract constructs and record those observations in a meaningful way so we can analyze the observations and draw the most accurate conclusions possible about our theories and hypotheses. When trying to find the best

http://dx.doi.org/10.1037/0000192-010
Selecting and Describing Your Research Instruments, by K. S. McClure
Copyright © 2020 by the American Psychological Association. All rights reserved.

instrument to assist us in observing and describing, there may be some barriers. In this chapter, I identify some common barriers and describe potential solutions to overcome them.

YOU CANNOT FIND AN INSTRUMENT

Sometimes the instrument you are looking for does not exist. It has not been invented yet. Although it may feel frustrating to discover this, it is also exciting because it may mean that you are studying something new or in a new way. When this happens, you can develop a measure of your own. If you choose to do this, I strongly suggest consulting closely with your advisor. Depending on the goal and scope of your study, you may be able to develop a simple instrument to observe and describe the construct. Alternatively, you may wish to revise your aims and hypotheses a bit so that you can study something similar that does have an available instrument.

NONE OF THE INSTRUMENTS ARE QUITE RIGHT

You can measure a construct several ways in the same study. Remember that you are trying to measure an abstract construct, and none of the instruments are going to be perfect. If there are two or three that are pretty good measures, use two or three of them in your study. You will have to run your data analyses twice if you use two measures and three times if you have three measures. You can then compare the results of your different analyses. If you do this, you should report all the results and explain the benefits and drawbacks of each measure. You also should compare and contrast the results from the different analyses by discussing how they are similar or different and why you think this may be so. We all want to think our hypotheses are correct, and it may be tempting to report only the results that support your original hypotheses, but you should not do that. That would go against the ethical principle of fidelity or honesty. Furthermore, if the results turn out to be different when the construct is measured different ways, it may be an interesting finding and something new that you discovered.

ACCESSIBILITY IS A BARRIER

Sometimes the intended sample has some specific accessibility needs and there is not an instrument that addresses those needs. In these instances, it is best to consult with experts on the particular accessibility issue and attempt to modify the format of the instrument so that the barrier to completing the instrument is removed. It is also a good idea to pilot any instrument modifications you make before collecting the data for your study.

LANGUAGE IS A BARRIER

Other times, the instrument will not be available in the primary language of your participants. You can consider having the instrument translated. Do this with great care and caution. Translations should always be done by a professional translator who is trained on how to translate for this particular purpose. Even if you are multilingual and can translate between languages, you should not translate your own research instruments. Sometimes there is not an adapted version of an instrument. If that is the case for your study, be sure to note that as a limitation in the discussion section of your paper.

THE INSTRUMENT HAS MULTIPLE SUBSCALES

You should always understand how an instrument is scored before you choose to use it. As I mentioned earlier in this book, some instruments have more than one score. They may have a total score based on the entire measure and then a few (usually three to five) subscale scores that are calculated by only using the responses to a subset of the items. These subscale scores also have particular meanings and measure parts of the construct. For example, a measure of problem solving may have a score for overall problem-solving ability and a subscale score that measures parts of problem solving, such as defining problems and brainstorming (D'Zurilla, Nezu, & Maydeu-Olivares, 2002). You do not have to use all the scores in your analyses. You can choose to only analyze the overall score or the subscale scores (or even just a few of the subscale scores). You make this decision by thinking carefully about the abstract construct you are trying to understand and study and choosing the score of the instrument that best observes and describes that construct.

YOU CANNOT FIGURE OUT HOW
TO SCORE THE INSTRUMENT

Always make sure you understand how to score an instrument before you decide to use it in your study. It is difficult enough if you think you want to use an instrument and the scoring is confusing or you cannot seem to locate instructions on how to score it. But at least you have the option of choosing another measure if you think you will not be able to figure out the scoring. It is stressful if this happens after you have already collected the data, so try to avoid that scenario. Commercially published instruments come with scoring instructions and a manual. The scoring instructions for instruments in the public domain are usually in the article where you found the instrument. If the instructions are not in the article or you need a little help understanding them, you can e-mail the corresponding author. The corresponding author's name and e-mail address are usually on the first page of an article, either above or below the abstract. The scoring instructions for instruments that are owned by the developer may or may not be in the article where you found the instrument. As with instruments in the public domain, look in the article first and then contact the corresponding author if needed. Remember that you will be contacting the corresponding author for permission to use the instrument, so it would be a good idea to include both requests in the same e-mail to save you and the author time. Figure 9.1 provides a sample email for requesting scoring information.

YOU CANNOT CONTACT THE AUTHOR
TO OBTAIN PERMISSION

When it comes to selecting instruments, I really do not like it if I am unable to contact the author when I have to do so. Luckily, it does not happen often, but it can occur. If you were a musician and found the

Dear Dr. [*insert last name here*]:

I am a student at [*insert name of university*]. I am designing a study on [*insert name of the general topic*], and my advisor's name is [*insert name of advisor*]. I plan to use the [*insert name of the instrument*] to measure [*insert name of construct*] in this study and already received permission from [*either remind the person that he or she granted permission for use or indicate from whom you received permission*]. Before I use the instrument, I want to be sure that I understand how to score it. However, I have not been able to locate this information. Would you be able to send me information about how to score this instrument? Thank you in advance for your time.

Sincerely,

[*insert your first and last name*]

Figure 9.1

Sample email requesting scoring instructions.

perfect guitar sitting in the studio, and you looked and looked for the owner but just could not find them, you would not take the guitar to the stage and play it anyway. The same is true for psychometric instruments. If you cannot get permission, you should not use the instrument. If you find yourself at a dead end and simply cannot track down the owner or get them to respond to your email, you may have to choose a different instrument even if you think another instrument is not quite as good. Before you come to this conclusion, though, consult with your advisor to make sure you have tried everything.

THE INSTRUMENT IS TOO EXPENSIVE

If the instrument is too expensive, let the instrument owner know. There may be student discounts. In addition, you could pursue a grant to cover the cost of the instrument. Your department or professional organizations may offer student research grants. Talk to your advisor about how to pursue a student research grant. Grants take time, so you should start this process early. Professional organizations can provide specific guidance and resources for psychology students. PsiChi, The International Honor Society in Psychology, offers over $400,000 in grants and awards annually, including spring, summer, and fall undergraduate research grants, as well as the Mamie Phipps Clark Diversity Research Grant for studies on diverse populations and issues. You can find more information at https://www.psichi.org.

I strongly encourage you to apply for a grant if you can. If you cannot find a grant or do not have the time to submit a grant application before the research project is due, you may have to choose a different and less expensive measure. I made this decision for my dissertation, and the study still turned out well and was even published in a professional journal. As long as the instrument measures the construct you are studying and has good psychometric properties, it is okay to choose an instrument because it is less expensive.

YOUR LIBRARY DOES NOT SUBSCRIBE TO THE RESOURCES YOU NEED

Sometimes you will identify a journal or book you think contains copies or descriptions of instruments you think will be useful in your study, but your library does not own the journal or book. This can happen for a variety of reasons. Library subscriptions are expensive, and library staff must choose their subscriptions or holdings carefully. Priority will often be given to journals and books that serve the most people in that community. For example, medical schools may subscribe to a range of medical journals, whereas liberal arts universities without a medical school may not. Depending on the topic you are studying and the type of community you are studying in, your library may or may not own a lot of the journals you need. However, when you need a journal article or book that your library does not own, refer back to the advice in Chapter 3 about consulting your librarians. You may be able to secure the resource you need through a simple interlibrary loan request. If not, the librarians can usually still help you get the materials you need. I have yet to meet a librarian who gives up before the article I need can be found.

YOU KEEP PROCRASTINATING AND CANNOT STAY FOCUSED ON THE TASK

What is a research and writing project without procrastination and distraction? I use several strategies to manage procrastination and distraction. The first strategy is acceptance. Over the years, I have learned to accept that procrastination and distraction are going to happen as long as I am a researcher. Now when I notice myself procrastinating or doing something other than working when I am supposed to be doing research, the first thing I do is think to myself, "Oh, there they are! Procrastination and distraction are back."

A second strategy I use to manage procrastination and distraction is thought reframing. *Reframing* is a strategy for adjusting unhelpful thoughts so that they are less unhelpful or so that they even become helpful. Some common unhelpful thoughts that lead to distraction are "I can't do this," and "My idea isn't very good." These thoughts make us feel down and less motivated to keep working. Reframing these thoughts to thoughts such as, "I'm having trouble, but there must be someone who can help me" or "Every idea has strengths and weaknesses; I put together a good team, and now may be a good time to consult them" can help you feel more positive and also motivate you to keep working.

Third, I use a category of behavioral management strategies to manage procrastination and distraction. This may sound technical, but the strategies are simple and include breaking the tasks into small parts, scheduling small and manageable working sessions (20–40 minutes at a time, at most), taking breaks, and rewarding yourself. It will not work well to block out several hours to sit down and select your instruments in one day or one afternoon. Give yourself a few weeks of short blocks of time. Reward yourself after each small accomplishment. I plan small blocks of time for research and put them in my electronic calendar. Then I write a list of what I plan to accomplish during each block of time that week. After each block of time, I reward myself with a nice big check mark (I have even resorted to putting stickers on my calendar for really unpleasant tasks). Then after larger accomplishments—for example, after I meet all of my research goals for the week—I download one song into a playlist so that by the end of the project, I have a nice playlist to enjoy if I accomplish all my goals.

Sometimes I write down the time I begin working and then jot down 15-minute increments for an hour. For example, if I begin working at 2:00, I will write on a scrap paper 2:00, 2:15, 2:30, 2:45, 3:00. Then I begin working, and after 15 minutes, if I have been doing what I set out to do, I put a check next to 2:15. If I have not been doing what I set out to do, I write down what I was doing (e.g., scrolling through social media). This keeps me accountable and forces me to look at how I am spending my time. Fifteen minutes later, I do the same thing, and usually, by then, I can put a check next to the time. I do not like to write down things more than once that I did not want to be doing. Figure 9.2 is an example of a behavior checklist for staying on task.

My final tip for managing distractions is to know yourself. Everyone has times of the day when they can stay more focused. For me, it is early in the morning. If you can, try to schedule your work for the time of day when you can focus most easily.

YOU HAVE SO MANY RESPONSIBILITIES THAT YOU CANNOT FIT THIS IN

One thing that can be difficult about completing a long-term research project is that it takes a lot of time. Most of us try to tackle large projects by carving out large blocks of time to work on them. This makes sense, but it is not practical, and it is also not the most efficient way to complete a large project. Instead, find small blocks of time (15–45 minutes) several times per week and put them on your calendar as if they are an appointment you cannot miss. Figure 9.3 provides a sample schedule that includes a five-class, 15-credit schedule of day classes plus a part-time job on some afternoons. If you would like more guidance about how to schedule yourself, especially for writing, I recommend *How to Write A Lot: A Practical Guide to Productive Academic Writing, Second Edition* (Silvia, 2019).

After setting a research schedule like the one in Figure 9.3, make a detailed list of what you have to accomplish and start scheduling those

Goal: complete the Possible Instruments Note-Taking Template for one instrument

Time	Did I work on goal?	If not, what was I doing?
11:30	No	Reading e-mail
11:45	✓	Good job
12:00	✓	Good job
12:30	No	Checking Instagram
12:45	✓	Good job—goal met ☺

Now you complete a behavior checklist:

Time	Did I work on goal?	If not, what was I doing?

Did this checklist help you notice when you were off task? Did it help you get back on task?

Figure 9.2

Behavior checklist example.

tasks into the blocks of time in your appointment calendar. This is the hard part. Most people will be tempted to schedule more than they can accomplish in a 15- or 45-minute period. Only plan to do what you can accomplish and no more. For example, if you are at the stage of your study when you are writing your institutional review board (IRB) application, for the Monday morning 9:00–10:00 research time slot, you may

Sample Research Schedule

	Monday	Tuesday	Wednesday	Thursday	Friday
9:00–10:00	Research	Class	Research	Class	Research
10:00–11:00	Class	Class and break	Class	Class and break	Class
11:00–12:00	Class	Study	Class	Study	Class
12:00–1:00	Lunch	Lunch	Lunch	Lunch	Lunch
1:00–2:00	Class	Research	Class	Research	Class
2:00–3:00	Go to my job	Class	Go to my job	Class	Go to my job
3:00–4:00	Go to my job	Class and break	Go to my job	Class and break	Go to my job
4:00–5:00	Study	Study	Research	Study	Reward myself for sticking to my schedule

Figure 9.3.

Sample research schedule.

plan to write a description of one instrument for your IRB application. That may be all you have time to do in one 1-hour block of time. The best-case scenario will be if you finish what you planned to do in a day with 5 extra minutes to spare. That will make you feel great. It will also make it more likely that you will work that efficiently the next time you sit down to the task. If you take 30 minutes to develop a plan like this, you will be able to see exactly what you have to do to finish the project.

I like to use a free app called Trello (https://www.trello.com) to make my lists. This app is like an online bulletin board that allows you to organize lists. The lists are laid out so you can see multiple lists at once, and you can drag items to different lists if needed. I create my project timelines on a Trello board with one column for each task or one column for each due date that I set. Then I list the to-do items in each column. If I do not complete a task, I move it to the next list, but this allows me to see that if I move too much to the next list, I will not complete the next list either.

In that instance, I have to rethink how I will finish the project. I may have to find one more 45-minute block of time per week to work on it, scale back the project, or extend the deadline if possible. You do not have to use Trello. If you want to use technology to manage your lists, you can use any list or note-taking function or application, such as Apple Notes or Microsoft Outlook OneNote. You can also write the lists on loose-leaf paper or in a paper planner. The lists just have to be in an organized format that you will refer back to and can modify as needed. If you put together your plan and see that you do not have enough time to complete the project, talk to your advisor about it at their earliest convenience. Your advisor may be able to help you make some adjustments so that you can accomplish your goal.

One final tip I have in this area is to use the last 3 to 5 minutes of each work period to record where you are leaving off, making a note of where to begin the next time, saving all your electronic files in an organized manner, and putting everything away where it belongs. This will help you get started easily and quickly and will prevent procrastination when you return to this task the next time.

In this chapter, I discussed all the issues my students and I have encountered. You may come across a new problem I did not discuss. After coming this far in the instrument selection process, you are prepared to address it, and you can turn to your advisor for support.

SUMMARY

This chapter described all the main categories of problems my students and I have encountered when trying to select and describe instruments for our psychology research studies. You will likely run into one or more of these problems as well. You may also encounter problems that are not in this chapter and that I have not thought of or encountered. I hope this chapter helps you feel prepared to respond to those problems effectively when they occur so that you can keep your project moving.

Conclusion

Selecting the best instruments for your psychology or social science research study and describing them effectively for your intended audiences are essential components of good research design. Just as a musician will not reach for the closest instrument on stage when playing a song simply because that instrument will play the song, you will not use the first instruments you find simply because they measure what you want to study. It is my hope that after reading this guide you feel better prepared to engage in a decision-making process that will allow you to select the best instruments for your specific studies. It is also my hope that you feel confident in the knowledge and skills you have to describe those decisions to your advisor, research team, institutional review board (IRB), and others who will collaborate with you and read your work.

Now your Advisor Consultation Checklist (Figure 1) is complete. We covered a lot of information in this brief guide. First, Chapters 1 and 2 discussed some general concepts related to instrument selection. These included identifying constructs and variables as well as types of instruments and the psychometric properties of reliability and validity. Next, Chapters 3 to 5 addressed the information-gathering process. This included the practice of identifying available instruments using library databases and search engines, books and book chapters, and searching within articles.

http://dx.doi.org/10.1037/0000192-011
Selecting and Describing Your Research Instruments, by K. S. McClure

It also included details about the types of information researchers have to gather about each instrument and how to record and organize good notes to refer back to that information throughout the research design process. The information-gathering phase also addressed the tasks of securing permissions to use instruments and using pilot data to inform decisions about instruments. Next, Chapter 7 addressed ethical guidelines and how they apply to instrument selection, and Chapter 8 explained how to describe instruments for the main audiences that will read your work.

The final chapter of this guide, Chapter 9, was on troubleshooting. Urban and van Eeden-Moorefield (2018) noted in their concise guide, *Designing and Proposing Your Research Project*, that research is an iterative process. This means that the process repeats, building on itself after each repetition. The researcher collects information, makes decisions, goes back and collects more information, makes more decisions, and so on. Instrument selection is an iterative process as well. It begins with identifying the constructs, continues through troubleshooting, and then returns to the process where needed. You may find that you have to go back through the process I described in this guide a few times until you make your final decisions about which instruments to use. Make more copies of the worksheets and fill them out again. It is important to allow yourself the time to do this because once you begin collecting data, you cannot go back and change your mind about the instruments.

Now is a good time to reflect on what you learned about the process of selecting instruments for research. What knowledge did you acquire? What skills did you practice? What organizational skills did you learn and practice? What consultation and collaboration skills did you learn to work effectively with your advisor and team? What did you learn about making research accessible to all people? I hope you will continue doing research and that you will feel both confident and capable of selecting the best research instruments the next time around. I also hope that your organizational and consultation skills will be useful in any setting and that your awareness of and sensitivity to accessibility will have a positive impact on the people with whom you work.

I also hope you had some fun. Parts of the process will be tedious and boring. Parts will make you feel anxious. However, it is exciting to create your own study, so if you are not having fun with it despite some of the difficult parts, you may be having a bit of trouble. Your advisor or team is there to help, so keep leaning on them. They will not know that you are having difficulty unless you tell them. When you seek their advice, be specific. Instead of making a general statement such as, "I'm overwhelmed" or "This isn't working," try explaining exactly what is wrong. For example, if you missed several of the goals on your timeline, explain that. Tell them what your goals were. If you do not know what got in the way of meeting those goals, ask your advisor or team for help identifying what got in the way. If you know what got in the way, share that information as well and ask for help in solving how to meet the goal.

I hope you found some great instruments to use in your study. I also hope you feel confident about moving on to the next steps in designing your study. Most likely, the next steps will be formally proposing your study, obtaining permission from the IRB, and collecting data. You might take a look at *Managing Your Research Data and Documentation* (Berenson, 2017). I wish you all the best as you continue your study.

SUMMARY

On a final note, the following are my main tips for you as you embark on the process of instrument selection:

- understand the constructs and variables you are studying,
- gather thorough information about the instruments that measure these constructs and variables,
- use your library resources (including the librarians),
- take detailed notes,
- organize yourself early and often,
- regularly consult with your advisor,
- remember the code of ethics,
- remember the multicultural guidelines,
- know that troubleshooting is part of the process, and
- have fun!

Glossary

CATEGORICAL VARIABLE   A variable that is described or measured in discrete or distinct categories (Chapter 1).

CLINICAL CUTOFFS   Ranges of scores that correspond to levels of mental health symptom severity or diagnoses (Chapter 8).

CONFOUNDING VARIABLE   A variable that may make it difficult to understand the results of a study because it also helps to explain the relationship between the two variables of interest by offering an alternative explanation as to why the variables are related (Chapter 1).

CONSTRUCT   "A complex idea or concept formed from a synthesis of simpler ideas" (https://dictionary.apa.org/construct; Chapter 1).

CONTINUOUS VARIABLE   A quantitative variable that, in theory, has an infinite number of values indicating the quantity or how much of the construct is present or reported (Chapter 1).

DEMOGRAPHIC VARIABLE   A variable that describes personal characteristics about an individual (e.g., age, race, religion; Chapter 1).

DEPENDENT VARIABLES   The variables that are thought to be affected by the independent variables in an experiment (Chapter 1).

HYPOTHESIS   A proposition based on a theory or some limited evidence about the frequency of a phenomenon or how two more variables are related (Chapter 1).

Important vocabulary terms are defined in this section. Each definition is followed by a cross-reference to the chapter where the term is first used and defined.

INDEPENDENT VARIABLES   The variables that are manipulated or measured first in an experiment to test how they influence the dependent variables or variables (Chapter 1).

INSTRUMENT MANUAL   A document describing the main characteristics of a psychological instrument such as the structure, scoring and interpretation, and psychometric properties (Chapter 6).

MAIN VARIABLES   The variables related to the study's aims and hypotheses (Chapter 1).

META-ANALYSIS   A quantitative technique used to synthesize the results of studies that have already been conducted by conducting a mathematical analysis of the effect sizes of the studies (Chapter 1).

OPERATIONAL DEFINITION   The specific method by which a variable is observed and measured in a particular study (Chapter 1).

PRIMARY SOURCE (for an instrument)   A manuscript that reports the original study about an instrument, such as the development and properties of the instrument (Chapter 3).

PSYCHOMETRIC PROPERTIES   The data, mainly regarding reliability and validity, that have been collected about an instrument to help us understand how well the instrument measures the construct (Chapter 2).

RELIABILITY   The consistency with which a construct is measured across various contexts and/or populations (Introduction).

RESEARCH AIM   The purpose or objective of a study (Chapter 1).

RESEARCH INSTRUMENT   A tool used to observe and describe psychological phenomena in a way that provides data that can be analyzed (Introduction).

RESEARCH METHOD   The methodical and scientific process a researcher uses to answer a research question (Introduction).

RESEARCH QUESTION   A broad question about the topic that the researcher is studying (Introduction).

SECONDARY SOURCE   An article or book that may include a description of the instrument, but that is not the main purpose of the publication (Chapter 3).

SYSTEMATIC REVIEW   A type of literature review that includes a synthesis and summary of research on a particular topic to draw a new conclusion (Introduction).

VALIDITY   The accuracy with which the instrument measures the construct it is designed to measure (Introduction).

VARIABLE   "A condition in an experiment or a characteristic of an entity, person, or object that can take on different categories, levels, or values and that can be quantified (measured)" (https://dictionary. apa.org/variable; Chapter 1).

References

American Psychological Association. (2010). *Publication manual of the American Psychological Association* (6th ed.). Washington, DC: Author.

American Psychological Association. (2017a). *Ethical principles of psychologists and code of conduct* (2002, Amended June 1, 2010, and January 1, 2017). Retrieved from http://www.apa.org/ethics/code/index.aspx

American Psychological Association. (2017b). *Multicultural guidelines: An ecological approach to context, identity, and intersectionality.* Retrieved from http://www.apa.org/about/policy/multicultural-guidelines.pdf

Antony, M. M., Orsillo, S. M., & Roemer, L. (Eds.). (2001). *Practitioner's guide to empirically based measures of anxiety.* New York, NY: Springer.

Appelbaum, M., Cooper, H., Kline, R. B., Mayo-Wilson, E., Nezu, A. M., & Rao, S. M. (2018). Journal article reporting standards for quantitative research in psychology: The APA Publications and Communications Board task force report. *American Psychologist, 73,* 3–25. http://dx.doi.org/10.1037/amp0000191

Baldwin, S. A. (2018). *Writing your psychology research paper.* Washington, DC: American Psychological Association. http://dx.doi.org/10.1037/0000045-000

Beck, A. T., Steer, R. A., & Brown, G. K. (1996). *Manual for the BDI-II.* San Antonio, TX: The Psychological Corporation.

Berenson, K. R. (2017). *Managing your research data and documentation.* Washington, DC: American Psychological Association.

Carlson, J. F., Geisinger, K. F., & Jonson, J. L. (Eds.). (2017). *The twentieth mental measurements yearbook.* Lincoln, NE: Buros Center for Testing.

Cronbach, L. J., & Meehl, P. E. (1955). Construct validity in psychological tests. *Psychological Bulletin, 52,* 281–302. http://dx.doi.org/10.1037/h0040957

D'Zurilla, T. J., Nezu, A. M., & Maydeu-Olivares, A. (2002). *Manual for the Social Problem-Solving Inventory-Revised.* North Tonawanda, NY: Multi-Health Systems.

Eid, M., Nussbeck, F. W., Geiser, C., Cole, D. A., Gollwitzer, M., & Lischetzke, T. (2008). Structural equation modeling of multitrait-multimethod data: Different models for different types of methods. *Psychological Methods, 13,* 230–253. http://dx.doi.org/10.1037/a0013219

Emery-Tiburcio, E. E., Mack, L., Lattie, E. G., Lusarreta, M., Marquine, M., Vail, M., & Golden, R. (2017). Managing depression among diverse older adults in primary care: The BRIGHTEN program. *Clinical Gerontologist, 40,* 88–96. http://dx.doi.org/10.1080/07317115.2016.1224785

Ethics. (n.d.). In *Merriam-Webster.* Retrieved from https://www.merriam-webster.com/dictionary/ethics

Evenson, K. R., Goto, M. M., & Furberg, R. D. (2015). Systematic review of the validity and reliability of consumer-wearable activity trackers. *The International Journal of Behavioral Nutrition and Physical Activity, 12,* 159. http://dx.doi.org/10.1186/s12966-015-0314-1

Gotlib, I. H., & Hammen, C. L. (Eds.). (2015). *Handbook of depression* (3rd ed.). New York, NY: Guilford Press.

Hamilton, M. (1960). A rating scale for depression. *Journal of Neurology, Neurosurgery & Psychiatry, 23,* 56–62. http://dx.doi.org/10.1136/jnnp.23.1.56

Hempel, S. (2020). *Conducting your literature review.* Washington, DC: American Psychological Association.

Kelley, M. L., Reitman, D., & Noell, G. H. (Eds.). (2003). *Practitioner's guide to empirically based measures of school behavior.* New York, NY: Springer. http://dx.doi.org/10.1007/b100496

Kroenke, K., Spitzer, R. L., Williams, J. B. W., & Löwe, B. (2009). An ultra-brief screening scale for anxiety and depression: The PHQ-4. *Psychosomatics, 50,* 613–621.

Lovasz, N., & Slaney, K. L. (2013). What makes a hypothetical construct "hypothetical"? Tracing the origins and uses of the 'hypothetical construct' concept in psychological science. *New Ideas in Psychology, 31,* 22–31. http://dx.doi.org/10.1016/j.newideapsych.2011.02.005

MacCorquodale, K., & Meehl, P. E. (1948). On a distinction between hypothetical constructs and intervening variables. *Psychological Review, 55,* 95–107. http://dx.doi.org/10.1037/h0056029

Markman, E. S., McClure, K. S., McMahon, C. E., Zelikovsky, N., Macone, B. W., & Bullock, A. J. (June 18, 2019). Social problem solving and posttraumatic growth new possibilities in postoperative breast cancer survivors. *Journal of Clinical Psychology in Medical Settings, 26,* 1–9. http://dx.doi.org/10.1007/s10880-019-09641-3

McNair, D. M., Lorr, M., & Droppleman, L. F. (1992). *EdITS manual for the Profile of Mood States*. San Diego, CA: EdITS.

Nangle, D. W., Hansen, D. J., Erdley, C. A., & Norton, P. J. (Eds.). (2010). *Practitioner's guide to empirically based measures of social skills*. New York, NY: Springer. http://dx.doi.org/10.1007/978-1-4419-0609-0

National Commission for the Protection of Human Subjects of Biomedical and Behavioral Research. (1979). *The Belmont report: Ethical principles and guidelines for the protection of human subjects of research*. Retrieved from https://www.hhs.gov/ohrp/regulations-and-policy/belmont-report/read-the-belmont-report/index.html

Nezu, A. M., Nezu, C. M., Felgoise, S. H., McClure, K. S., & Houts, P. S. (2003). Project Genesis: Assessing the efficacy of problem-solving therapy for distressed adult cancer patients. *Journal of Consulting and Clinical Psychology*, *71*, 1036–1048. http://dx.doi.org/10.1037/0022-006X.71.6.1036

Nezu, A. M., Ronan, G. F., Meadows, E. A., & McClure, K. S. (Eds.). (2000). *Practitioner's guide to empirically based measures of depression*. New York, NY: Springer.

Radloff, L. S. (1977). The CES-D Scale: A self-report depression scale for research in the general population. *Applied Psychological Measurement*, *1*, 385–401. http://dx.doi.org/10.1177/014662167700100306

Ronan, G. F., Dreer, L., Maurelli, K., Ronan, D., & Gerhart, J. (2014). *Practitioner's guide to empirically supported measures of anger, aggression, and violence*. New York: Springer. http://dx.doi.org/10.1007/978-3-319-00245-3

Silvia, P. (2019). *How to write a lot: A practical guide to productive academic writing* (2nd ed.). Washington, DC: American Psychological Association.

Tavakol, M., & Dennick, R. (2011). Making sense of Cronbach's alpha. *International Journal of Medical Education*, *2*, 53–55. http://dx.doi.org/10.5116/ijme.4dfb.8dfd

Tedeschi, R. G., & Calhoun, L. G. (1996). The Posttraumatic Growth Inventory: Measuring the positive legacy of trauma. *Journal of Traumatic Stress*, *9*, 455–471. http://dx.doi.org/10.1002/jts.2490090305

Urban, J. B., & van Eeden-Moorefield, B. M. (2018). *Designing and proposing your research project*. Washington, DC: American Psychological Association. http://dx.doi.org/10.1037/0000049-000

Index

About the Author

Kelly S. McClure, PhD, is associate professor and chair of psychology at La Salle University in Philadelphia, Pennsylvania. She received her doctorate from Drexel University in 2002. She was a coeditor of *Practitioners Guide to Empirically Based Measures of Depression* and is currently an associate editor of *Clinical Psychology: Science and Practice*. Her main research interests are social problem solving and coping with cancer.

About the Series Editor

Arthur M. Nezu, PhD, DHL, ABPP, is Distinguished University Professor of Psychology, professor of medicine, and professor of public health at Drexel University. He is currently editor-in-chief of *Clinical Psychology: Science and Practice*, as well as previous editor of both the *Journal of Consulting and Clinical Psychology* and *The Behavior Therapist*. He also served as an associate editor for both the *American Psychologist* and the *Archives of Scientific Psychology*. Additional editorial positions include chair of the American Psychological Association's (APA's) Council of Editors, member of the advisory committee for APA's *Publication Manual*, and member of the task force to revise APA's journal article reporting standards for quantitative research. His research and program development have been supported by the National Cancer Institute, the National Institute of Mental Health, the Department of Veterans Affairs, the Department of Defense, the U.S. Air Force, and the Pew Charitable Trusts. Dr. Nezu has also served on numerous research review panels for the National Institutes of Health and is a member of APA's Board of Scientific Affairs. He is previous president of both the Association for Behavioral and Cognitive Therapies and the American Board of Behavioral and Cognitive Psychology and the recipient of numerous awards for his research and professional contributions.